LINKING THROUGH DIVERSITY

Practical Classroom Activities
for Experiencing and
Understanding Our Cultures

Edited by
Walter Enloe and Ken Simon

Zephyr Press
Tucson, Arizona

Linking through Diversity
Practical Classroom Activities for Experiencing
and Understanding Our Cultures

Grades K–12

© 1993 by Zephyr Press.
Printed in the United States of America

ISBN 0-913705-88-8

Editors: Stacey Lynn and Stacey Shropshire
Design and Production: Nancy Taylor
Cover Design: Nancy Taylor

Back Cover Photo: *BoTrain* by Kambia Conteh of Sierra Leone.
Photograph from *See Me, Share My World*, a global education
project of Childreach. Used by permission.

Zephyr Press
P.O. Box 13448
Tucson, Arizona 85732-3448

Library of Congress Cataloging-in-Publication Data

Linking through diversity : practical classroom activities for
experiencing and understanding our cultures / edited by Walter Enloe
and Ken Simon.
p. cm.
Includes bibliographical references.
ISBN 0-913705-88-8
1. Intercultural education—United States—Activity programs.
I. Enloe, Walter, 1949- . II. Simon, Ken, 1958- .
LC1099.3.l56 1993
370.19′6′0973—dc2092-40687

CONTENTS

PREFACE

The world is more and more of a neighborhood, but is it any more of a humanhood? Unless we learn to live together as brothers and sisters we shall perish together as fools!

        —Martin Luther King, Jr.

This book grew out of teachers making connections between places and peoples. For me it began at Hiroshima International School, where I was teacher and principal from 1980 to 1988. The international City of Peace and Culture was a natural place from which to begin making exchanges with my students' home schools and countries. It was also a natural nexus for linking the world's children through the 1000 Crane Club, whose story is told in chapter 10.

In 1988 I came to the Global Education Center at the University of Minnesota to work with John Cogan, who had been a visiting Fulbright professor at Hiroshima University in 1983 and 1984. Working in a global education school transformation project, I began meeting or hearing of educators who believe in experiential, interdisciplinary learning and projects and who were making living connections with other places and peoples, going beyond themselves and expanding their "classrooms."

From the Paideia School in Atlanta, where I taught for nine years, to Rhode Island and school communities in Minnesota and Wisconsin, I found teachers who were willing to tell stories about their children's building, exploring, and researching the world. I thank all these people for exemplary teaching, for enhancing the experiences of young people by helping them bridge the local and the global and by turning the seemingly mundane or trivial into active, creative, stimulating, and integrated learning topics and projects. Thanks especially to Ken Simon, my coeditor, a colleague and friend, for the partnership. Thanks also to Roger Wangen, Bob Wedhl, and Wayne Erickson at the

Minnesota Department of Education for supporting our original project.

In 1988 I began a partnership with the Redwood Falls School District on the western plains of Minnesota in the county of "Little House on the Prairie." I was director of the Minnesota in the World Project, the rural component of the National Model Schools Project in Global Education, which asks communities to determine what attitudes, skills, and knowledge graduates need to live as healthy citizens of the twenty-first century. In Redwood Falls the community then asked, "How do we most effectively help our students acquire the appropriate attitudes, skills, and knowledge? What practices, programs, and organizations do we need to implement to facilitate their acquisition?" One goal of Redwood Falls educators is to ensure that graduates understand the world and its peoples, locally and globally, as interconnected and interdependent. This book represents a contribution to that goal; thanks especially to the Blandin and Bremer Foundations for ensuring the project's success.

The mediums of experience, we argue, are primary messages. Building upon the counsel and work of John I. Goodlad, Redwood Falls and other school communities have developed a blueprint for school development. Through the active mediums of interdisciplinary, integrated, international, and interpersonal learning, students and their teachers will learn through, and not only vicariously about, the ecological and cultural webs in which they are embedded locally and globally.

We want to thank Zephyr Press for empowering educators to be creators. We especially thank Stacey Lynn and Stacey Shropshire for their editorial support, encouragement, and collegiality.

This book is dedicated to the life work of Jean Piaget; to our colleagues, friends, and mentors Charlotte Anderson, John J. Cogan, and Anna Ochoa; to the citizens of Redwood Falls and Kake, Japan; and to teachers and children in the Hands across the Seas Project.

WALTER ENLOE

INTRODUCTION

Culture is the widening of the mind and spirit.
—Jawaharlal Nehru

We do not intend this book to be a typical teacher's manual. We have included no lesson plans with objectives and neatly sequenced activities, though one could construct them from each article. What we offer in these pages is a window into the classrooms of teachers who provide activities that support multicultural and global education.

Though a standard teacher's manual is useful to teachers, there exists a void of manuals that deal with issues as powerful as multiculturalism and globalism. That void can be filled when teachers find opportunities to communicate and exchange ideas and beliefs. This book is but one way for teachers to engage in such conversations and exchanges.

A number of assumptions underlie this project:

• The world is increasingly interdependent, complex, and changing.

• We may think and act globally, but we are locally embedded ecologically and culturally.

• An ecological paradigm is becoming more prevalent in human thought. An educator needs to choose between thinking predominantly in a mechanistic manner (viewing the brain as an information processing machine) or thinking in an organic (open) manner. Many

1

teachers tacitly take a mechanistic approach. We choose the organic perspective.

• An organic systems worldview has a corresponding pedagogy: interactive, interdependent, integrative, interdisciplinary, international, and interpersonal.

• Interconnections exist between intercultural, cross-cultural, international, multicultural, and global concepts, and we need to understand the interconnections before we use any of the concepts.

• People, especially children, are active learners. They are essentially active creators, experimenters, and explorers. Children can be scientists: anthropologists, archaeologists, economists, historians, psychologists, sociologists, environmentalists, and ecologists.

• Knowledge and truth are communal. We need to cooperate and collaborate in order to operate fully.

• People are communicators. Teachers and children can write books.

• Children can be teachers; teachers can be learners.

• We have proved that the old saying "There are those who do, and there are those who teach" can be modified: "There are a lot of us who *do* teaching."

• The great teacher, like great students, is collegial, self-evaluative, open, competent, and creative; the great teacher practices hard and well and is a perpetual learner.

• After traveling through the United States, a British teacher remarked, "There are more cultural differences between Minnesota and Tennessee than there are between Boston and London." In our multicultural nation, we need to link locally, regionally, and nationally, as well as internationally. Too often teachers think in terms of "strange lands and friendly peoples." Instead, this book builds on the present, the immediate past, the commonplace, and the local as stepping-stones to the globe.

• We are all global educators. We use interconnected meanings when we speak of "a global education" and "a global perspective of education." We are speaking (1) of or about globes; (2) about world interdependent systems such as ecology, communication, economy, and technology; (3) about world issues: global warming, global poverty, nuclear destruction, disease, and so on; (4) about Spaceship Earth; (5) about the global family in the global village; and (6) about sphericism and holisticism.

Why do we use *intercultural* rather than *multicultural, global,* or *international* as the theme of this project? There are several reasons, but the most important is that we are striving for an interconnected "feel" in the classroom. We can have multicultural classrooms that consist of children from many different cultures, but they may not be interacting and learning to understand one another. The term "intercultural" suggests interacting in a way that increases the understanding and respect we have for our many cultures.

1

A CASE FOR CREATING THE INTERCULTURAL CLASSROOM

by Dorothy D. Hoffman

For the world is not to be narrowed
'til it will go into the understanding
but the understanding is to be expanded and opened
'til it can take in the image of the world.

—Francis Bacon

The challenge of creating the intercultural classroom pales in comparison to the overriding, general challenge of formal K–12 education—the challenge of preparing students for "life the other side of age 18." A large portion of this task can be subsumed under the duty of helping students to make sense of the world in which they live. If a student doesn't master this ability, the world can be a bewildering and intimidating place, a place with which a student will likely not want to interact and from which he or she may want to escape or withdraw, adopting behaviors incompatible with democratic values and with those values necessary to a healthy, happy life.

To make sense of the world, students need knowledge and the skills to interpret that knowledge, but they also need the will, the courage, and the persistence necessary to complete the process of understanding. To achieve this goal, they must see this process modeled by adults who are important in their lives. Teachers are among the most significant of these adults.

In today's age, "making sense of the world" requires knowledge of much that is international and intercultural. The prospect of teaching material that is not part of the "traditional" curriculum, a curriculum that already requires near-manic creativity and "fast-forward" teaching, could coax more educators who are eager to escape the profession over the proverbial edge into real estate, lawn service, and the consultation of other educators. But we can view intercultural education as an opportunity as well as a challenge: If we can integrate intercultural and international content into existing curricula, it can facilitate students' learning of nearly all traditional material.

Students are often aware of the many interconnections among people of the planet but lack a thorough understanding of both the genesis and implications of these interconnections. Piaget believes that children possess "a spontaneous belief that everything can be explained by everything else" because everything is connected to everything else. Children come to formal education curious about, interested in, and connected to all other people. From the child's earliest exposure to formal education through his or her post-secondary experience, however, the system often works to erode this interdependent construct. It does so, largely inadvertently, through the fractionalization of the curriculum into subject areas, a one-nation and one-gender approach to history and the interpretation of history, we-they studies of culture, teacher-centered delivery of information, and schooling that is largely isolated from world reality. Students are often left on their own to synthesize the information they learn.

> *If we can integrate intercultural and international content into existing curricula, it can facilitate students' learning of nearly all traditional material.*

Many movements are afoot attempting to reform this system, movements promoting changes in philosophy, methodology, and content that, if implemented, can nurture, rather than be at odds with, the interdependent construct. Whole-brain learning theory, concern for learning styles, cooperative learning structures, interdisciplinary teaching, literature-based reading programs, increased emphasis on problem solving in all disciplines, and the whole-language approach to language arts are but a few examples. In the intercultural classroom, the educator uses a combination of the above methods to bring students "to the heart of things," calling upon their senses, minds, souls, and spirits to help them interpret the world in which they live. Ultimately, the goal is to develop whole-minded students who are interested enough in the world to want to understand it and confident enough to want to interact with it.

Intercultural education is also education that increases interest in the world in which we live. At the core of such a curriculum curiosity must reside, curiosity that manifests itself in an environment rich and deep with words, colors, faces, textures, stories, and close, close looks at the very small and the very enormous; an environment of awe, wonder, and wander that both touches and invites touch. It is an environment that encourages the four-year-old in all of us to continue to ask questions. Such a curriculum is one that provides a warm and receptive hearth for the "Why?" and "How?" and "From where?" and "Maybe . . ." and "What if . . .?" questions and responses of students and their teachers. It is a curriculum that builds students' awareness that they live in a universe, a universe they share with all things and forces, living and nonliving. The following poem expresses this sense of wonder:

The School of Names
NANCY GOFFSTEIN

I want to go to the school of names
to know every star
in the sky I can see
at night
I want to know what's in the ocean
every school of fish
every watery motion
by name

I want to know
every stone and rock
crystal—shale
granite—chalk
every kind
by name

Names of continents
seas
islands
mountains
shores
deserts, rain forests
and the grasses, flowers, trees and bushes
growing on the earth

How are the winds called?
What are the names of the clouds?

I want to go to the school of names
to know everybody
with me
on this globe

every mammal
reptile, insect
bird, fish and worm

I would like to recognize and greet
everyone by name
For all the time I may live
no place
but the earth
is my home.

For the teacher, creating the intercultural classroom means
finding materials and creating situations through which students can
study a variety of perspectives. I have found that materials appear

everywhere: political cartoons and maps; letters on the editorial page; articles about the Japanese internment camps, Colombia's view that the United States must fight the "war against drugs" from the domestic demand side of the issue rather than the imported supply side, the world debt situation from the vantage of a developing country, U.S. sugar subsidies and their effect on the Dominican Republic, the destruction of Brazil's rain forest relative to its national debt, the voyages of Christopher Columbus from several points of view; cartoonist Gary Larson's portrayal of humans from the perspective of animals; and many others.

Looking at current events through the eyes of the political left, center, and right encourages the kind of analysis students will have to repeat almost daily if they are to be thinking voters. Understanding even a few of the basics of how Christians, Moslems, Hindus, Buddhists, or atheists might view a given situation could be extremely helpful to making sense of today's world. Simulations provide excellent exercises in understanding perspectives. Cooperative learning structures, of course, increase exposure to the perspectives of students' classmates and provide opportunities for cooperation within the diversity to be found there.

Additionally, intercultural and international content makes the educators' task of assisting students in making sense of the world one with which students can more readily identify because such content resonates with the reality the students perceive. A study void of intercultural content presents but an illusion of today's world, and many students will recognize it as such. Basically, if you enhance the importance of a concept, your students are likely to learn it more readily.

The intercultural curriculum is one in which students are familiar and comfortable with being asked to think critically and to problem solve creatively. One of the most important questions is "How did it get to be this way?" because the history of every person and every thing is essential to understanding fully that person or thing. To really "know" a frog is to know its ancestors, its evolutionary history. To "know" Minnesota is to know its story from preglacial to current times. An individual's life story includes the stories of those whose genes she or he carries.

There are several different ways to reinforce the traditional curriculum with intercultural material, such as data, examples, analogous information, and so forth. For example, if those studying the American Revolution were to study briefly other revolutions past and present, those students would likely not only understand the concept of revolution, but because of the many examples and the comparative study, the American Revolution itself would become more relevant to the students' views of the world. In a similar way, students may cherish the U.S. Constitution more if they compare it to the constitutions of other nations and see that many other nations have used our constitution as their prototype. Teaching the elements of a folktale by examining tales from five cultures or nations is more instructive and likely more interesting than focusing on one area's folktales. Such parallel study also helps students add a new dimension to that which they cherish as their own.

If all you teach is interesting, students will learn more easily that all has worth. Such teaching also provides a link to a second essential component of the intercultural curriculum: An intercultural curriculum is one that provides an image of the humanity and value of every person on Earth, an image students acquire by learning more, accurate information about him or her. It is an education that makes other people "real" to students—not "the same," not always people or individuals with whom we agree, but people who have value. I think Thornton Wilder knew of this importance and perhaps shared the mission of the intercultural classroom when he wrote in *Our Town* in 1936:

> Rebecca and George had readied themselves for bed and were engaged in one of those child-to-child conversations that carry great weight and wisdom:
>
> *Rebecca:* George, is the moon shining on South America, Canada, and half the world?
>
> *George:* Prob'bly is.

Rebecca: I never told you about that letter Jane Crofut got from her minister when she was sick. He wrote Jane a letter and on the envelope the address was like this: It said:

Jane Crofut; The Crofut Farm; Grover's Corner; Sutton County; New Hampshire; United States of America.

George: What's funny about that?

Rebecca: But listen, it's not finished. The United States of America; Western Hemisphere; the Earth; the Solar System; the Mind of God—that's what it said on the envelope.

George: What do you know!

Rebecca: And the postman brought it just the same.

In analyzing my own style of international teaching I realized that the elements that follow in this essay were those I hold closest to me—those I deem essential to the intercultural classroom. These elements usually can be integrated easily into the existing curriculum, requiring little more than a change of focus, a modified questioning strategy, or an alteration in the style of a presentation.

Older students respond positively to, and often are truly amazed by, the adults who still "wonder" publicly and with enthusiasm.

In the elementary classroom opportunities with which to engage students in curious explorations abound. Young students are still enthusiastic, and nearly every story they read can provide intercultural content if an educator who possesses intercultural curiosity presents the story. Older students respond positively to, and often are truly amazed by, the adults who still "wonder" publicly and with enthusiasm. In addition to the teacher's being a positive, curious role model, challenging curiosities are presented in the writings of every field of study. Lewis Thomas excites wonder exquisitely in *The Lives of a Cell,* as does Loren Eiseley in *A Journey through Time.* Teachers searching for learning materials with high "curiosity quotients" will begin to find them in unlikely places and will begin to see many

11

opportunities for infusing curiosity into otherwise unprovocative material.

People think, feel, and behave the way they do in response to their immediate familial contexts as well as to the larger cultural, historical, and sociopolitical context in which they live. Attempting to understand this context on a personal-to-international continuum can mean the difference between sympathy and empathy, disdain and compassion, intolerance and tolerance, isolation and communication, and war and peace.

In addition to the physical, emotional, intellectual, and spiritual characteristics shared by the species, humans also share commonalities in the structures and institutions they create and sustain. The intercultural classroom is one that approaches the study of cultures through the universal elements present in all cultures. Students asked to brainstorm a list of the elements of culture they would expect to find if they were dropped into a village anywhere on the planet will generate a list and a categorization of the list that is very similar to one that a cultural anthropologist would generate. The list can provide a structure for studying cultures, others' and a student's own, throughout the K–12 experience. With intercultural study reinforcing the traditional curriculum, students will see that the concepts of culture they are learning are not only relevant to their lives but are applicable to, and as wide as, the world.

Families are basic to all cultures. Although family configurations show many variations, their function is fundamental—to nurture, to support, and to be supported by. Lullabies sung in thousands of different languages transmit the same comfort and security. Nursery rhymes entertain and teach similar lessons. All children are affected by their relationships to their families, and healthy and abusive practices are distributed globally.

Neighborhoods, communities, and cities exist in all cultures and were established in geographically similar locations, for similar reasons, to perform similar functions. Inquiry at all levels, "discovered" by the students, yields data about the importance of harbors, confluence of river systems, nearness to boundaries of geographic transition, climate, topography, and so on, in the placement of world cities. Well- and ill-planned cities and sections of cities exist in all nations, just as people of upper, middle, and low income exist in most cities, although the percentages in each category vary substantially. Students may be curious about the universality of this phenomenon and deserve honest answers: The causes of poverty are also universal.

Children, having first learned about their own families or neighborhoods or communities, are fascinated with the diversity to be found within the sameness of a given function. Through such study they should be able to recognize family, neighborhood, and community wherever it exists, and in populations of animals other than humans as well.

Similarly, a study of the basic human needs (food, shelter, clothing, clean water, love, and esteem) and how people everywhere strive to meet these needs allows students to view people of other cultures without condescension. These needs, when seen from an anthropological point of view and taught through inquiry methodology, become fascinating real-life problem-solving opportunities. "If you were to live on this island, at this latitude, at this altitude, with this vegetation, with this much rainfall, and these average seasonal temperatures, what might you eat? From what materials might you build your home? Where will your cities be built? What will citizens of your island do for work? For recreation? What might you export? What might you have to import?" Through this process, a hut, shack, or shanty becomes home; a sari, a logical choice of dress; and fufu, cola nuts, or kangaroo, sensible foods to eat. Students see that people's choices are very similar to those choices students themselves would make if the students were in parallel settings.

We can give students hypothetical settings and ask them to design a culture for a particular latitude and biome and can then ask them to compare it to an actual culture in that latitude and biome. In intermediate and secondary study, case studies of particular cultures allow students to discover how all the universal elements are expressed uniquely in each culture. Here, we can integrate study into all curriculum areas as students explore the language, monetary systems, social and political organization, literature, art, religions or belief system, rites of passage, education, and so forth, of each.

Students who are exposed to photographs, folktales, films, lullabies, games, songs, dances, poems, and a range of stories from many people and cultures will recognize the elements we all share, those that designate us as members of the human race. The capacity to feel joy, sadness, fear, anger, despair, compassion, and ecstasy, and the capacity to contemplate the future, life, death, and afterlife, all link humans one to another.

> *The capacity to feel joy, sadness, fear, anger, despair, compassion, and ecstasy, and the capacity to contemplate the future, life, death, and afterlife, all link humans one to another.*

For the sake of analogy, cultures can be compared to trees. Cultures, like trees, are rooted in their history, the collective experience of their past; this history and the environment in which children find themselves growing determine what their "trunks" and "bark" look like and how they present and organize their "leaves" to manufacture their sustenance. Each cultural tree is decorated differently and nurtures its offspring in a manner peculiar to itself. Although all cultures are "trees" and possess the same or similar parts, the diverse ways in which they manifest "treeness" is truly fascinating.

One method of studying various cultures is to take an intercultural approach to one of the universal elements. Longfellow International Fine Arts School in Minneapolis used corn as the theme for a year-long, schoolwide study. Students traced the genetic development of the plant, made time lines and maps of its spread from Central America to the rest of the world, researched the folklore and mythology of corn, discovered the different forms of corn as food for both people and animals, and prepared tortillas and mush and grits and polenta and corn bread. They grew corn and dissected it to learn about its life cycle. They used corn for multiplying—rows times number of grains per row. They used "Indian" corn in classification activities. Staff and students learned more about corn than they knew was possible, and the theme provided us with an example of how rich a seemingly simple topic can be.

I've always wanted to research four or five of the world's most basic food grains and have the students, from the raw form, grind and otherwise prepare those grains to make them into whatever forms are used in particular areas of the world. Most grains are used to make breads (often both leavened and unleavened), porridges, graincakes, some type of fermented liquid, pasta, or dumplings, and are also used for thickening. Mapping activities and recipe collecting could accompany such exploration.

Educators could choose a universal element for each grade level to explore. For example, fourth graders could explore shelter and look at how this basic need is provided for in many different geographic and cultural areas of the world. Another grade level could explore clothing, another dance, another family structures and lineage patterns, and so on.

Every child, everywhere, deserves reverence from someone who holds that child sacred.

Every child, everywhere, deserves reverence from someone who holds that child sacred. Being a parent has made me a better teacher and a more compassionate human being. I can look at a child and know how wonderful is the depth to which he or she is loved, or conversely, I can know how profoundly tragic it is that he or she is not loved deeply enough. Or that in spite of the depth of love a parent feels for a child, that parent is unable, because of whatever circumstances, to convey to the child the safety that love and competent parenting provide. But the value is still within the child whether the child is cherished or abused by people or by fate, because I am convinced that children come to Earth not only through their parents.

Students, having been exposed to the shared humanity of many peoples, can come to realize that children born onto earthen floors can be as cherished, and as healthy, as those born in the most elite of hospitals. The tenth child can be as loved as the first. A parent in Thailand who "sells" his daughter to the factory owner so that she will be fed and there will be more food for the remainder of his family most likely cares intensely about that child. The humanity of individuals is not always reduced by poverty, or by extreme wealth, and it certainly is never totally eradicated.

Students will obviously become aware that all children, regardless of their intrinsic value, are not treated equally by family or by fate. Alice Walker in *The Temple of My Familiar* describes a character as follows:

> . . . and a shapely, sun-brown woman with a look of the most intense anticipation of good on her face. It was a face that expected everything in nature to open, unresistingly, to it. A face that said Yes, not once, but over and over again. It was one of those faces that people have when they've been sufficiently kissed as very young babies and small children. (278)

If a child realizes that he or she has not been, or is not being, "sufficiently kissed," the child can be helped to know that he or she deserves to be, and that it is not the fault of the child that he or she is not. Studying the "United Nations Convention on the Universal Rights of the Child" not only makes children aware of the rights they, ideally, should possess, but also, if taught in a personalized manner, could give a child license to be sad about not owning them and can affirm his or her right to find someone to talk with who will treat him or her with the dignity and respect the document says every child deserves. UNICEF and state United Nations Associations have additional materials for use with primary, intermediate, and secondary children.

There are many books, lessons, and songs that teach of the value, or breach of value, of human beings, but perhaps the most compelling of those lessons are those the child experiences firsthand in the classroom. A healthy classroom environment that fosters positive student-to-teacher and student-to-student relationships is perhaps the best teacher of the value of human beings.

If each person is valued, and students know that cultures share many elements that are the result of unique adaptations to geography and history, the next step in the intercultural classroom is to help students understand the perspective of other individuals and groups of individuals. Exploring a perspective does not mean taking that perspective oneself or agreeing with that perspective. Learning about the perspective of others can lead to a life made richer by a variety of interpretations and perceptions.

Maya Angelou had this to say about perspective in an address delivered in Minneapolis on January 15, 1987, Martin Luther King, Jr.'s birthday:

> *I am a human being. Nothing that is human is alien to me.* This quote is attributed to Terance. In the encyclopedia you will find after his name "Terentius Afir, 154 B.C." He was not born white. He was not born free, and he became Rome's most popular playwright. Now if you take his advice, decide not to separate yourself from other humans—this decision is a serious one. It means if someone takes a Mack truck, runs over babies in the street, commits the most heinous crime, you can never again say, "Oh I could never do that!" Not if a human being did it. You must rather say, "I mean never to do that. I intend to use my energies constructively rather than destructively. But if a human being did it, I have within myself all the components to do that thing, and let me not separate myself from the human being."
>
> On the other hand, if a human being paints a portrait, paints a great painting—a Picasso, a Matisse, an Elizabeth Cattlin, a Mary Cassatt—that seems to reach under your rib cage and lift you up, it means you have within you the possibility of doing that thing. If a human being writes a piece of music—a Mozart, a Verdi, a John Louis—if a human being writes it, you have it within you. . . . If a human being dares to love somebody and has the unmitigated gall to accept love in return, it means you can do it too. That's what it means. Now I know that's liberating!

Much of learning can be described in terms of learning new perspectives. Much of humans' quality thinking is actually a comparison of perspective, and much of health and happiness is finding and owning one's own perspective. Understanding another's perspective can widen a path, broaden and deepen vision, increase choice, unbind a spirit, and open a mind and heart.

Educators are not so naive as to think that such understanding will lead to the absence of conflict. Sometimes understanding the perspective of another could lead more quickly to conflict, if the person's or nation's perspective is one that is threatening to another individual or nation. But knowing how another thinks and the context that created this thinking would likely be a great help in dealing with him or her. This knowledge could also decrease the duration and destructiveness

> *Understanding another's perspective can widen a path, broaden and deepen vision, increase choice, unbind a spirit, and open a mind and heart.*

of a conflict. Conflict created by contrast in perspectives can also be used as fodder for helping students learn how to deal constructively with conflict.

Exposure to and acceptance of such diversity will help the student find and accept his or her own diversity, his or her own perspective. "Helped are those who love and actively support the diversity of life; they shall be secure in their differentness."

The intercultural classroom is, additionally, one that illustrates the interdependence of the planet's inhabitants, its human and nonhuman populations. Although all systems of the Earth seem to have globalized far faster than have the mechanisms and laws to deal with them, and many seem to hang in a perilous state, it is the global environmental system that has recently received so much attention—perhaps because all other systems necessarily interact with, and actually depend upon, this system, or perhaps because, as was so clearly conveyed in a Pogo cartoon, "For centuries we have been doing to the Earth; now it is doing back." I am constantly reminded of the profound warning in the Lakota prophesy that states, "Whatsoever befalls the Earth befalls the sons and daughters of the Earth." Scientists predict that as many as fifteen million plant and animal species will become extinct in the next fifteen years. And remember that in diversity lies the preservation of the planet.

Sunderlal Bahungane is founder of the Chipko or "tree hugger" movement in India. When forests were threatened by "development," villagers and farmers literally tied themselves to trees to turn back the bulldozers. Bahungane tells this story:

> Would you like to know what has happened to the trees? A pygmy was running with a big tree under his arm. Somebody asked, "Where are you going?" He replied, "To find a safe place for the tree!" The next question: "Of what are you afraid?" His reply: "The cement road is following me."

Industrialized societies with market economies put roughly fifty to seventy-five times the pressure on the Earth's biosphere as do traditional societies. In thinking about the "opening" of Eastern Europe

It is very important to present students with a balance of the hard realities and the valuable gifts of interdependence.

and the increased need for zinc, copper, steel, wood, and healthy waste management, I see an image of the Earth sighing.

Exploring other interconnections and linkages may not produce such sober discussion as does the global environment. In learning of any of the interconnections of Earth's inhabitants, however, and keeping in mind that the overarching goal of international or intercultural education is to reduce the intimidation of our students, we must exercise caution. It is very important to present students with a balance of the hard realities and the valuable gifts of interdependence. Mr. Rogers, with whom I doubt many of the global education "experts" have consulted, has provided an analogy of sorts. In one of his weekly columns, Mr. Rogers described how babies sometimes induce a feeling of rejection in their caregivers when the babies abruptly change their expression, look away, or bury their heads in someone or something that blocks their vision. Mr. Rogers assures caregivers that this behavior is not rejection but rather a way for the babies to take a rest from what he calls "sustained looking" and that the rests are usually brief. Before long, babies are once again gazing at the faces of their closest caregivers. Mr. Rogers goes on to say,

"Both taking in and shutting out are important throughout our lives. Just as the capacity of sustained looking is important for learning, so, too, the capacity for shutting out can help us cope with the stimulations and stress of everyday life."

The message? Intercultural education can occur daily, but we must learn to take in and shut out so as not to burn out—so as not to intimidate, to cause despair or guilt, to spawn denial—so that our students will come back to the issues with which they must wrestle to ensure a habitable future.

We can also combat burn-out and intimidation by emphasizing the positive and joyous aspects of interdependence. There are songs and rhythms and instruments to discover; games to be played; fabrics, dyes, weaving machines, and a billion patterns and designs to admire. There are nuances of language to learn, folk dances to dance, trees to hug, spices and flavors to enjoy, pottery and wooden bowls to hold, and prayers to hear. Through all of these we can learn more about others and, perhaps the greatest benefit, learn more about ourselves.

Learning about others and ourselves brings us to the final point. The intercultural classroom is one in which the individual is helped to understand him- or herself and his or her relationship to the global reality. Learning multitudes of information means little if that information isn't integrated into one's being and then reflected in one's behavior. Students made curious about the world and having learned to understand and accept the value and perspectives of others are more likely to be curious about, to understand, and to respect themselves. These elements support students in the development of their "owned" orientation toward important issues and in the formulation of their own worldviews. We must give students opportunities to think critically and along diverse and unfamiliar lines about nearly all of what they study so they can develop their own opinions, their own ideals, and their own philosophies. Such opportunities are also the means to students' personal power and confidence, the means to ward off intimidation and powerlessness, to develop courage.

Looking, confronting, leaves an "open" where the "closed" was. Going about in the world, seeing it as it is, is a much better way to spend one's time than in hiding. We can go about in the world best if we are at home within ourselves. The Good Witch in *The Wiz* explains: "Home is a place we all have to find, child. But it's not just a place where we eat or sleep. Home is knowing your mind, knowing your heart, knowing your courage. If we know ourselves, we are always at home anywhere." And the following is the last entry in Anne Frank's diary:

> Is it true that grownups have a more difficult time than we do? No. I know it isn't. Older people have formed their opinions and don't waver before they act. It's twice as hard for us young ones to hold our ground, and maintain our opinions, in a time when all ideals are battered and destroyed, when people are showing their worst side, and do not know whether to believe in truth and right and God.
>
> It's really a wonder that I haven't dropped all my ideals, because they seem so absurd and impossible to carry out. Yet I keep them, because in spite of everything I still believe that people are really good at heart. I simply can't build up my hopes on a foundation consisting of confusions, misery and death. I see the world gradually being turned into a wilderness, I hear the ever-approaching thunder, which will destroy us too. I can feel the suffering of millions, and yet, if I look up into the heavens, I think that it will all come right, that this cruelty too will end, and that peace and tranquility will return again.
>
> In the meantime, I uphold my ideals, for perhaps the time will come when I shall be able to carry them out.

We must help our students to be interested in the world, to understand it better, to find the courage to search for and own their ideals, for the time has come to carry them out.

2

LETTING THE OUTSIDE IN:
TEACHING FROM THE COMMONPLACE

by Peter Ames Richards

*Curious how little impression experience too familiar makes upon
. . . minds, how little attention is paid to it. With an oversecure,
not to say ridiculous, contempt . . . are we despising everyday
experience, we specialists and half the world besides.*

—Charles Sanders Pierce

I graduated from college having been taught, in those previous sixteen years, more about the common landscape and culture of past or
foreign civilizations than I was taught about my own, present-day
culture and landscape. By the end of college, for example, I'd learned
about the classic Greek agora, the ancient marketplace, but not about
the shopping centers fringing the newly "developed" suburban
sprawls of the 1950s.

My own observations of vernacular architecture (diners, super-
markets, gas stations, the new interstates, the ubiquitous strips) were
never reinforced or given stature by any of my teachers. Moreover,
no one had taught me how to observe, to read the common landscape, to become interested in the history of everyday products or

> *The . . . world . . . is a rich, mostly untapped resource for exciting, innovative teaching that not only validates children's experiences but also urges them to become active, curious observers of their environment.*

objects. People assumed then (as they continue to assume today) that children will naturally observe the world around them and ask questions about it—but not as part of a classroom lesson. Except for a current events club and some moldy word problems in math, the real world was ignored, never used as a learning resource. As far as school was concerned, the outside world didn't exist.

Perhaps this lamentable separating of schools from the outside is a throwback to medieval academies, where monastic islands of education kept learning alive in oceans of chaos. We don't today, however, live in the Middle Ages. The outside world, still chaotic but perhaps safer, is a rich, mostly untapped resource for exciting, innovative teaching that not only validates children's experiences but also urges them to become active, curious observers of their environment.

Research projects that reach out from the classroom and make contact with the "real" world also touch the lives and experiences of students, involving them powerfully. Such projects utilize the same academic skills as traditional schoolwork. Instead of teaching time-rate-distance equations using a textbook, with its imaginary towns and schedules, for example, you can teach the same equations by giving each student a copy of, say, the current Delta Airlines schedule. Which is more relevant? Which is more interesting? Which really teaches survival skills? (Also, and this is very important, real timetables are not only free, they're exciting, full of promise.) Students want competence and control over the world and recognize useful information when they see it: timetables, schedules, 1040 forms, menus, road maps, real-estate guides, and application forms.

The Turf Map

One way to begin an examination of the everyday is to have children draw "turf maps." I define *turf* as the area around one's home where most playing, hanging out, and exploring takes place. It's an area in which one should feel safe, secure.

The best way to understand a turf map is to draw one yourself. Perhaps you can go back in time to when you were ten or so. Think of the area around your home, your turf. Think of the boundaries of that territory: a river, a big highway, a fence, bullies, whatever. Were all the boundaries defined by landscape features? Were the boundaries determined by your parents?

Having established your boundaries, fill in the map. Your home need not be in the center of the map, nor does your map have to be square or rectangular. Some people like to work from their home outward, adding sheets of paper when necessary.

Scale doesn't matter and you need not draw everything in. This experience is meant to be nonthreatening. Houses don't even have to look like houses. Bullies' homes can loom larger than they were.

Here are some other elements on a typical turf map:

> dogs and other animals
> dangerous, scary places; mean people
> watercourses, lakes, ponds, puddles
> landscaping created by children (bike trails, forts)
> trees (climbing, fruit), gardens
> best friends
> stores
> the best hiding place ever
> places where you had accidents
> places endowed with mythic properties
> seasonal activity areas (skating, sledding, baseball, football)

If your students draw such maps, what do they get out of the activity? First, the students begin to understand maps as representations of spatial reality, as communication of information. A map becomes a two-dimensional re-creation, a personal aerial view of memories and experience.

After your students have drawn the maps, it's important to share the maps with the class. Many of the turfs will overlap. Students will learn about each other. Such sharing also gives children a sense that their "whole selves" are welcome in school.

I would like to see all students draw yearly turf maps to be included in their permanent files. What a window on the experience of the child! What a remarkable way for schools to endow a child's experience with interest and credence!

You can expand the turf map exercise. Have your students' parents and grandparents draw turf maps of their childhood homes. How are the maps different from those your students draw? What would a turf map drawn by a person with a disability be like? How are urban turfs different from suburban or rural turfs? What maps would children in foreign countries draw? How does one's turf map change as one ages? The turfs will certainly expand with the ability to ride a bike or drive a car.

Daffodils along Route 1

One fall, close to Thanksgiving, I talked to my class of ten- and eleven-year-olds about the coming of spring. What, I asked, is the beginning of spring? Spring, some kids knew, begins March 21 (or so). I then asked them what object or occurrence conveys to them "SPRING"? Some responses: spring training for the major leagues, the first dogwood blossom, the first daffodil, bags of grass seed in hardware stores, Easter candy on market shelves.

We decided that the first blooming daffodils would provide a way to measure the coming of spring for our project, which was to answer the questions, "How fast does spring move from south to north along the East Coast? How could we find out?"

I showed my students Route 1, the first interstate, on a road map of the eastern United States. I explained that, because it had an odd number, Route 1 was a north-south highway (even-numbered interstates run east-west). Route 1 starts in Key West, Florida, and ends up, nearly 2,800 miles later, in Fort Kent, Maine, hard on the Canadian border. Route 1 was a convenient path to use to follow spring up the coast.

How could we follow the first daffodils, those golden harbingers of spring, up Route 1? We needed correspondents. Some students already knew people who lived along the route. Those who didn't wrote to postmasters and -mistresses in small towns along the way, describing the project, asking for the names of people who might help, and enclosing a self-addressed, stamped postcard.

The postcards soon came back from the postmasters and -mistresses, and students started writing to their daffodil correspondents. They described our project and asked the correspondents to write the dates they saw the first blooming daffodils in their area on the self-addressed, stamped postcards we enclosed and to mail the postcards.

And then we waited.

School went on as usual, and then one day, a postcard arrived from Key West, from the Garden Club, reporting that daffodils never grow in Key West—it's too hot. That's something none of us had known.

Finally, a postcard from Santa Claus, Georgia, reported their first daffodil on February 1. We were on our way north on Route 1!

The cards trickled in, or sometimes we got a whole slew in one day. A woman in Aberdeen, North Carolina, sent a photograph of her grandson sitting next to the first daffodil. AAA maps on a bulletin board, showing the whole route, sprouted arrows and dates. The daffodils were marching north!

May 4, 93 days after we got the postcard from Georgia, Fort Kent, Maine, responded. We pored over road maps, trying to figure out the actual distance from Santa Claus, Georgia, to Fort Kent. Using a 1936 map, on which Route 1 was the only route, we found the distance to be 1,740 miles. Dividing that by the number of days, we got 18.7 miles a day, about .78 miles per hour. Spring creeps up Route 1 about a quarter of the speed of a walk!

What did the class learn from all this?

- How to write a letter and elicit information from a stranger (What a stimulus to writing a clear, neat, friendly letter!)
  - How to address an envelope
  - How to read a map
  - How to use mileage tables
  - How to use time-rate-distance equations

In one small project the students threw themselves into math, writing, geography—all good basic skills. None of those students will ever drive on Route 1 again and not think of that daffodil project and wonder about spring.

In the future we might do a frost study along Route 1, from north to south. We can use the same correspondents, perhaps. Perhaps we'll continue following blooming daffodils all the way into Quebec, discovering how far north they grow, having our letters translated by a high-school French class. There are any number of activities we can generate from this one idea.

Learning from the Yellow Pages

I used to work at a school that required teachers to teach "dictionary skills" in third grade. The textbook I was given, like most textbooks, was boring, and the boredom brought out the worst in my students. Frustrated, I thought about my own life: Did I use the dictionary much? Sometimes, but the dictionary I used most was the yellow pages of the phone book.

I admit, I'm a yellow pages nut. If I find myself in a new town or city and I really want to find out what the place is about, I don't read the tourist brochures on the bedside table; I read a local paper and the yellow pages. Look up churches, and you find out the religious makeup of a town. Look up restaurants, and you find its ethnic composition. Flip through the yellow pages and you see what trades, industries, and crops are important.

The yellow pages, besides being a time-saving reference book for consumers, can be an exciting, inexpensive resource for schoolchildren who are learning about the real world and acquiring important survival skills. As a historical document, the yellow pages can tell us a lot about a community: its values, history, geography, and even its climate.

The Atlanta yellow pages have only one listing for snow-removal equipment but twenty-four pages of listings for air conditioning. What does that tell us? How would it differ from the listings, say, of Minneapolis? Also in the Atlanta yellow pages, the first pizza listing (under "Pizza Pies") appeared in 1960. Today, there are eight pages of listings. What does that tell us about our taste in food? I wonder when sushi or hot tubs first made the yellow pages?

> *As a historical document, the yellow pages can tell us a lot about a community: its values, history, geography, and even its climate.*

The yellow pages, so much a part of our daily lives, can become a nonthreatening reference in school. As children use it in the classroom, their knowledge of the outside world will increase and the gap between school and home will diminish. Moreover, that particular learning will be reinforced every time they use the yellow pages on their own.

I like to introduce the yellow pages by asking my students who have telephones to bring in some old or new copies and then having the class skim through them. Students will find categories and occupations that will be new to them, see interesting advertisements, and perhaps recognize businesses. Perhaps there will be words that are new to the students. You might ask them to write, say, five questions that occur to them as they browse.

The local telephone company will be glad to provide you with free copies of the yellow pages for your class—delivered. Why? It's good business for them—they're introducing their product (essentially a catalogue of advertisements) to young people. I always order enough for all the students in the class and me and keep the books.

They last a few years, then I get a new bunch. Lately, however, I've had students who own telephones bring in their old yellow pages after they receive their new copies. Recycling the old books makes more sense than just asking for new ones.

After students have had this initial contact with these books, I might divide the class into large groups, perhaps eight or ten students in each group, and ask them, for example, to find the telephone number of the nearest McDonald's. Some students might look up the heading "McDonald's" instead of "restaurants." Now would be a good time to explain the difference between the white and the yellow pages. Perhaps one group will look up McDonald's under "restaurants." That's step one. Step two would be to find the *nearest* McDonald's. In a small town, it will be the only one listed; in a larger city, students might have to figure out which street address is closest to the school.

Think of all the reference ("dictionary") skills needed to answer that one question—finding the main topic, using guide words on top of the pages, spelling, alphabetizing, building vocabulary, and deciphering abbreviations. These skills are good and basic and all come from *one* exercise in the yellow pages, a reference book your students have seen hundreds of times. Your students are acquiring and using the same kinds of skills a workbook about a real dictionary would include. The difference is that the yellow pages are hardly threatening. Using them in the classroom is kind of fun, different. Because the books are so common, students' guards are down, and they really enjoy the activities.

After students become more familiar with the yellow pages, I like to use the books for "scavenger hunts." For this activity I provide sheets that have ten to fifteen questions that the students can answer by using the yellow pages. As students become more familiar with the book and develop strategies and expertise, I make the groups smaller and smaller until the students are working individually. Sometimes, I give a time limit. Students can do the work in school or at home, where, of course, most people have a copy of the yellow pages already. (If you have students who don't have telephones, you can allow them time to do their work in the library or allow them to check out a copy of the yellow pages to take home.)

Here are some sample questions I've used, working with the Atlanta yellow pages (*BellSouth Real Yellow Pages*):

• How many McDonald's <u>restaurants</u> are there on Jimmy Carter Boulevard in Norcross? What are their street numbers? (At first I might underline the listing word to eliminate premature frustration.)

• Which <u>baton twirling</u> instructor has two studios? In which towns are the studios located? What is the sum of their street addresses?

• How many Greek Orthodox <u>churches</u> are there in the Atlanta area?

• I want to buy a <u>chalkboard.</u> Which town has two companies that sell them?

• B. H. Produce is a company that sells <u>frozen food</u> wholesale. What is its motto? (Here, as with many questions, kids will have to find the listing, and then move to the large advertisement, which is sometimes on another page.)

• Which company outside the State of Georgia produces <u>fireworks</u>?

• Ken Stanton Music sells <u>pianos</u>. How many years has Ken Stanton been in business?

• Tile House is a <u>tile dealer</u>. They buy tile from several countries. Name two. What continents are the countries in?

When making up yellow pages questions, I have to be very careful to proofread them, making doubly sure that they are correct. There's nothing more frustrating to a child than an unanswerable question!

You can view the yellow pages as an unbiased primary source of information on our way of life. The telephone books are a cultural artifact, part of the commonplace, thus a possible and imaginative resource for teaching.

I run off ten or twenty pages of questions and use them for a slow time in a week or during recess on a rainy day. Sometimes I'll put all math questions on one sheet, all geography questions on another, and so on. Often I give prizes (usually doughnuts) for the teams that find the answers in the least amount of time.

You can expand this activity easily. Perhaps the local historical society has some old yellow pages. How would they compare? What do automobile ads look like from the 1950s? The 1920s? When did hot tubs, computers, FAX machines, and TVs first appear in the yellow pages? You can view the yellow pages as an unbiased primary source of information on our way of life. The telephone books are a cultural artifact, part of the commonplace, thus a possible and imaginative resource for teaching.

Fast Food

Of all the businesses in our country, the fast-food business is the most frequented by our students. They eat fast food and hang out in fast-food outlets. Some of the students work in outlets after school. All have seen fast-food TV commercials, which are specifically targeted to teenagers and children. I used the ubiquitous fast-food outlet as an interesting subject for a project that lasted, on and off, for three months. The project entailed writing about the history of a specific fast-food chain. In Atlanta, where I teach, there were enough fast-food chains to allow each of my thirty students to choose a chain without having any two students researching the same chain.

Once my students chose their chains, we brainstormed questions that had to be answered in their reports:
- Where was the first outlet?
- When did it begin?
- Who started it?
- How did that person get into the fast-food industry?
- How many outlets are there?
- Where are they?

• How has the menu changed since the chain was started?

• When did particular food items come on line?

• What products have been eliminated from the menu?

• How has the architecture of the chain changed?

• What were the prices of the menu selections when the chain began?

Some of the questions posed were typical of business-school seminars:

• Why did the chain succeed?

• How did the personality of the founder create success?

• Why does the menu work (or not work)?

• Does the menu include different items in different places to reflect the culture of those areas (for example, does a McDonald's in Russia have some items that we don't have here)?

We stayed away from proprietary information on earnings, real cost of products, salaries.

How can these questions be answered? I asked.
Write the company.

How do we get the address?
Call a local outlet.

To whom do you write?
Most students want to write to the president of the chain, but then we talk about different administrative jobs in companies: planning, financial, quality control, and . . . public relations. You write to the public relations manager!

Why?
That's the job of a public relations person. She or he will get your letter eventually if you write the president, but why not cut out the middle person? (Already kids were learning something about how a company operates, learning some new vocabulary, problem solving, finding out facts that would be difficult to find in a library.)

The first piece of work, since most of the historical information would come from the company, was the letter. *What does a formal letter look like? How is an envelope addressed? Where does the stamp go?*

Putting together the letter took time. We talked about what kinds of letters would be most appreciated. In class meetings we often role-played a busy fast-food executive receiving a letter from a Paideia student. *What might touch a company official in such a way that he or she would reply promptly with information we could use? What did we need to establish rapport?* Perhaps a line about why one picked the particular fast-food chain: "I picked Burger King because I love grilled hamburgers and hate fried ones." "I picked Dunkin' Donuts because my father proposed to my mother in one." Perhaps the faceless official would appreciate an anecdote: "I remember when I used seven packages of ketchup to eat one hamburger. I love your ketchup." I told them about the *worst* letter ever sent: "Send me everything you can about Kentucky Fried Chicken."

Finally, the letters were finished, warm and friendly, in the students' best handwriting. Their envelopes sealed and stamped, my class flung their letters hopefully into the vast unknown of the fast-food industry, sent to strangers who knew them only by their written words and upon whose beneficence their projects would succeed or fail.

After the letters went out, we talked about additional questions that could be answered in students' reports by visiting a local outlet of the chain.

• *Architecture and design:* What are the primary colors of the chain? Draw a plan of the site, including parking, dumpster, landscaping, and entrances. Draw an interior plan, showing seating (booths or tables or both), traffic flow, plants, bathrooms, food preparation area. How many minutes can one sit in a seat and still feel comfortable? (We all know that fast-food and mall seating is designed to get you up and about within a short time.)

• *Ambience:* What are the colors and textures of the interior? What kind of music is played? What is on the walls? Is the traffic

flow appropriately suited to handle both eat-in and take-out custom-
ers? Is the place clean? What are the bathrooms like?

• *Manager:* I have each student interview a manager of a fast-
food outlet. I give a little talk about how to set up an interview, how
to come prepared, how to take notes, how to direct the interview. We
do role-playing exercises about interviewing. Some typical questions
to ask a manager include

> • How old are you?
> • How did you get into the fast-food business?
> • How many employees work here?
> • How many are full-time? Part-time?
> • What is the age range of employees?
> • Have there been any robberies here? Any accidents in the
>   parking lot? Any memorable occurrences, such as births,
>   deaths, marriages, famous people as customers?
> • What was the biggest order?
> • When does the place open? Close? What's the busiest
>   day? Time?
> • What qualities are important to being a manager
>   or employee?
> • What's the turnover of employees?
> • How are the bulbs changed in the outside sign?

The product of all this research, some of it done through the mail,
some of it by interview and observation, is a five-minute oral report
on the history of a student's particular chain. I've always had students present a poster, as well, displaying a picture of the first outlet;
a map of states or countries the chain is in; a picture of the founder;
examples of packaging, advertising, and giveaways from the chain;
photographs; an employment application (filled out by the student);
and other artifacts.

What have kids learned from all of this?

• How to write a letter
• How to conduct an interview

- How to take notes
- How to look at just another blot on the landscape and realize that it, too, has a history
- How to find history all around, not just in books, but on the commercial strip

As a class, we have constructed a time line, showing the years when fast-food chains began. We try to figure out the cluster years when many fast-food chains were starting. We talk about why fast food became so popular: the rise in the number of interstates, more two-job families with less time to cook, the lure of standardization, and so on.

We also put flag pins on a map of the United States showing where each chain was founded. We see that the Southeast and the Northeast were the birthplaces of most of the fast-food chains. Why is that? Why haven't fast-food chains been started in, say, Wyoming? Kids begin to see the country in terms of population density and other demographics, begin to see that fast-food chains depend on a lot of traffic, and begin to *understand* what they've always *seen*.

> *[There is] history all around, not just in books, but on the commercial strip.*

Most important, the information that kids have learned from their projects and those of their classmates will be constantly reinforced. They will never be able to drive mindlessly down a strip. Their minds will be remembering, observing, asking questions. They will be connected to their environment.

History Down the Supermarket Aisle

Another subject I've covered with my students involves each student in researching the history of an ordinary supermarket product. Let's say, for example, Jell-O–brand gelatin.

• What's the history of Jell-O? When was it invented? Who invented it? Where? Why? How is it made?

• Why do the directions say not to put fresh pineapple into Jell-O? What happens if you do?

• What did the packaging used to look like? How has it changed? What did early advertisements look like? When were the different flavors introduced? How has the price changed over its history?

• Can you make your own Jell-O with unflavored gelatin and fruit drink? Can you get it to taste better than Jell-O? (You could conduct blind taste-tests with the class.)

Think of the possibilities, just with Jell-O! Think of all sorts of different, everyday objects and products kids can research. How about toothpaste brands or cookies or cars or a stretch of commercial strip?

Conclusion

I've described a few projects that I've done with students eight to twelve years old. I know you can do the projects with older students, as well. You can probably think of dozens more ideas yourself. However, following are some warnings:

• Don't just jump into this stuff. Think about it, begin to collect materials, be sure of why you're doing it. If you get into it before you're ready, you know your principal is going to come up to you one day and say, "Mrs. Morris tells me you're studying Oreos." You'll need to know, right at that second, *why* you're doing such a study, why studying cookies is such a powerful subject, integrating all subjects. You must believe in it. Otherwise it's too risky; it doesn't *sound* like schoolwork, but you must be able to tell others why it certainly is.

• Don't overdo it. I have my class do projects like those I've described, but we also spend a lot of time with the multiplication table and rules for adding suffixes, all that regular schoolwork. And that's as it should be: Kids need to know how to use math and writing, how to talk and write about books. Learning from the commonplace is enrichment, the icing on the cake, not a year-long curriculum (although I did have one class study a fifteen-mile-long, mixed usage road for a year).

• There's no teacher guide. Some of these projects have all sorts of unexpected parts to them. You need to be flexible. Once, my class studied 400 feet of commercial strip in Cambridge, Massachusetts. Each kid had a store to investigate. In December, the man who ran the barbershop died. Now what? You've got to be able to handle unexpected circumstances.

• You need to take a risk. Studying part of our culture firsthand, without guides, is scary. You will be learning along with your students—a courageous act. You will be taking risks, but why not? Think of the risk-taking implicit for kids just to go to school. Maybe it's not such a bad thing to see the teacher taking risks, too.

Teaching from the commonplace is not only fun, but it also urges our students to look at their world closely and see that everything has a history; that someday their landscape will be historical; that, perhaps, people will pay to ride in an internal-combustion-engine car, just as weekenders pay to ride a steam train that goes in a loop without stopping. The clothing that your students wear to school could be in a museum 200 years from now. Even junk mail will be artifacts some day.

> *Think of the risk-taking implicit for kids just to go to school. Maybe it's not such a bad thing to see the teacher taking risks, too.*

When you can get children to see that what they consider boring commonplaces will become, some day, part of history, they will never be the same; they will then understand, as we all should, that they are actually living in history, that our life is the performance, not the dress rehearsal. If we can get children to really observe their world and give them the vocabulary to describe it, to appreciate it even, we have given them a tremendous gift. The risks are worth it.

3

LINKS ALONG THE
MISSISSIPPI RIVER

by Ken Simon

One of the marvels of early Wisconsin was the round river,
a river that flowed into itself, and thus sped around and around in
a never-ending circuit. Paul Bunyan discovered it, and the Bunyan
saga tells how he floated many a log down its restless water. No
one has suspected Paul of speaking in parables, yet in this instance
he did. Wisconsin not only had a round river; Wisconsin is one.
The current is the stream of energy which flows out of the soil into
plants, thence into animals, thence back into the soil in a never-
ending circuit of life. "Dust unto dust" is a desiccated version of
the round river concept.

—Aldo Leopold, *The Round River*

My entrance into the world of linking students happened by
coincidence and accident. A friend of mine had just taken a teaching
job in Khartoum, Sudan. Before she left I called to wish her well. In
the course of the conversation we talked about staying in touch,
which led to an idea of having a few of our students exchange letters.
A few weeks later another friend suggested that my friend in Sudan
and I exchange cultural artifacts. It was the beginning of a year-long
project; students exchanged letters, boxes of artifacts, and eventually
video letters. For my students who participated in the exchange, it
was an exciting learning experience that truly opened their eyes to a
distant culture. More than once, my students said they would like to
visit Sudan eventually.

What follows are ideas and suggestions for linking students, teachers, classrooms, and schools along the Mississippi River. I use the Mississippi only as a model for linking projects. There are certainly many other possible themes. But choosing a river is a highly personal act for me. The summers of my youth were spent canoeing the rivers of northern Wisconsin and reading the philosophies of people such as Aldo Leopold. I see the river as a metaphor for the interconnections, interrelationships, and interculturalness of our world.

Why Link along the Mississippi When We Can Link Internationally?

Though our link with Sudan was an important and meaningful experience for my students, it didn't quite resolve a problem of which I have been aware for several years. That is, in what ways will students truly learn about culture (not only understand culture as a concept, but also understand individual and specific cultures) without thinking culture is limited by national, political boundaries?

> *. . . linking needs to be a step-by-step process in which students learn about their own culture, those "other" cultures close to them, and then those cultures that are more distant and foreign.*

I realized the need to answer this question during my first year of teaching. One of the goals of seventh-grade geography classes was to have students learn about world cultures. To achieve this goal I gave my students a definition of the concept of world culture and fortified the definition with many texts and primary-source readings, as well as with movies and with discussions about cultures around the world. It wasn't until the review day for the final exam that I realized that the way I taught culture was a problem.

At the beginning of the review session I remarked that "of course we all know what culture is." It seemed like a harmless enough thing to say—culture had been the "focus" of the course (at least in my eyes). Then came the question: "Mr. Simon, I really don't understand what we're supposed to know about culture." It came from a bright and interested student, and it caught me off guard. As I thought about how to answer, she went on to say that she understood the definition of culture, but she wasn't sure how to apply that definition to all the places we had studied since they were all so different.

I eventually realized that the way I approached the teaching of culture didn't give students the tools they needed for multicultural analysis. Students in my seventh-grade geography class had learned various things about many cultures, but they never really had a chance to experience culture. My ninth graders, who linked with students in Sudan, were able to experience culture and become active learners. Their project turned them into archaeologists, scientists, and historians. But their experience with culture was limiting, as well. They viewed cultural differences as being distant and strange (foreign). They marveled at the strange foods that their Sudanese friends ate and at the types of houses the friends lived in. And since my students had never experienced as archaeologists, scientists, and historians the cultural differences within their own national boundaries, they viewed culture as something defined by present-day nation states, rather than as something defined by history, tradition, and need.

Linking is a wonderful tool for learning about culture. But to solve the problem with studying culture that I have stated, linking needs to be a step-by-step process in which students learn about their own culture, those "other" cultures close to them, and then those cultures that are more distant and foreign. The Mississippi River is but one model for designing links that address these problems.

The Mississippi River as a Link

Every night we passed towns, some of them away up on black hillsides, nothing but just a shiny bed of lights; not a house could you see. The fifth night we passed St. Louis, and it was like the

> *whole world lit up. In St. Petersburg they used to say there were*
> *twenty or thirty thousand people in St. Louis, but I never believed*
> *it till I seen that wonderful spread of lights at two o'clock that still*
> *night.*
>
> —Mark Twain, *Adventures of Huckleberry Finn*

I selected the Mississippi River as a natural link for a variety of reasons. One reason is that I now live and teach in St. Paul, Minnesota. The river is still a central part of the diverse cultures here. Yet an even more powerful reason has to do with the metaphors that a river conjures up. Rivers are the natural links between various ecosystems: swamps, valleys, forests, plains. The river also links people of various cultures—rural people, urban dwellers, farmers, and business people—as well as linking those people with the various ecosystems. And finally, the Mississippi has played an important part in the history of the people who have inhabited this continent and of this continent's natural environment.

Historically, the Mississippi River is a living repository of the human experience in North America. It represents the experiences of the Native Americans who fished its waters, grew food along the plains, and hunted the wildlife in the valleys. For some Native American groups the river is the subject of legends and tales that tell us of the philosophy and ethics of peoples who revered nature.

The river represents the experience of Africans who were brought to this country as slaves. Ironically, the river was at once a symbol of oppression and freedom to slaves. The waters of the river brought them on trading ships and irrigated the plantations. But the river also provided a means for slaves to reach freedom in the North. When slavery ended, many African Americans moved to the cities and towns along the river in search of a new life.

The Mississippi represents the experience of Europeans who built cities and factories along the river. One finds the artifacts of the ethic of progress along the river—an ethic that is tied to the desire to control nature. Each community along the 2,300 miles of river has its own distinct culture. One can find literally hundreds of different cultures at work.

The Mississippi River is but one means of linking students within a classroom, a community, and a nation. Other means of linking might include state and federal highways or interstates, train routes, and even routes of planes that fly out of your local airport. You might poll your students about where they have been within the state, the nation, and the world and establish links based on their experiences. The method you choose should fit your particular class or school needs.

Building the Link

I have designed this project for students in grades 6 through 8, though you can adjust many of the activities for students who are younger or older. Given the daily schedule of middle and junior high schools, some structural problems may exist. How does one schedule this project into a busy year and a full curriculum? Establishing links between schools can be time consuming. The project does not fit neatly into a three-week unit since the links need to be continuous throughout the course of a year, if not for two or three years.

Linking projects are flexible, however; your class can leave them and pick them up at various times throughout the year. The activities suggested here are designed as side dishes, not main courses. You can blend many of the activities into your normal curriculum, which will enhance it. You can budget your time based on the types of projects you and your students choose to undertake. I suggest that you set aside a few days a month for a project. In our links with Sudan, one day a month was enough to organize the materials that we sent. The video project took longer, but it served well as an excellent research, writing, and cooperative project.

Overall, the value of linking far outweighs any scheduling or curricular problems. My ninth graders who participated in the Sudan link had a better grasp of the specific cultures we studied in world history and were more motivated to learn about other cultures than those students who did not participate.

Cultural links need not be initiated only in social studies classes, either. Science, humanities, art, and math teachers can enhance their classes using links. Linking also offers a unique opportunity for inter-disciplinary activities. Using links, you can design activities that examine economics, history, and geography, as well as the various ecosystems, literature, art, and music of the culture with which you link. A social studies teacher might also want to link with a science or humanities teacher to assist on some projects.

> *Linking . . . offers a unique opportunity for interdiscipli-nary activities.*

The activities listed below are merely suggestions. Letting your students choose the activities they would like to work on is a great way for them to learn about group decision making as well as to develop a sense of democracy, trust, and responsibility for their actions. You and your students might have additional ideas for activities. Use them and let us know what you did and how it worked.

In the Beginning:
Uncovering Our Own Culture

The first stage of the project takes about three class periods and focuses on helping students understand culture through artifacts. Begin by introducing students to personal artifacts. The artifacts tell a story and act as a catalyst for discussion about the concept of culture. One way of introducing students to artifacts is to have students act as investigators who try to establish the identity of a person by using only the available artifacts.

I begin this game by bringing a box of personal items in a brown paper bag. I tell students that the artifacts belong to one person and that the students' job is to find out as much as they can about that person based on her or his belongings. Enhance the lesson by using your own artifacts. Some students may be able to figure out that you are the person. Here is a list of items in my box:

- one very dirty high-top Converse canvas tennis shoe
- one disposable razor head

- an old Bob Dylan T-shirt that reads "Dylan Concert, Omaha, 1971"
- a copy of *Canoe* magazine with dog-eared pages
- two books on ancient history
- a broken shaft of a canoe paddle
- an empty Head and Shoulders shampoo bottle
- a pair of cutoff khaki pants

I then have the students work in groups of three as they rummage through the artifacts. Each group makes a list of characteristics about the person. Once each group has completed a list, I make a class list on the board. Then I divide the list into categories such as physical features, interests, and habits. I have found that the class usually develops a good profile of the suspect within one class period. If students do not figure it out, I reveal to them that the artifacts are mine.

At that point we begin to discuss the idea of culture using the profile we just built. For homework, I have students choose ten artifacts to bring into class that would help someone else build a profile of them. Once they have chosen the artifacts, they will create a chart with three columns; the column headings are "item," "description," and "inference." The students list their artifacts, then write an objective description, and finally write what inferences can be drawn from their artifacts.

The next day in class I have each student trade artifacts with another student (pair students who don't know each other very well) and write a profile of the other person. Then the students work in pairs reading and discussing the profiles. The next part of the period can be spent discussing three topics:

- What can artifacts tell us about people in a specific place and time?
- What are the limitations of artifacts? (What can't they tell us?)
- Which artifacts were better than others and why? (In other words, which artifacts tell us more about the person?)

For homework that night, I have the students rank their artifacts from one to ten, one being the most important. I tell the students that their criterion for ranking is not whether they like the artifact the most but whether the artifact will best tell someone about their culture. I have them annotate this list, focusing on why they ranked each artifact as they did.

On the third day, the students work in large groups, at least six to a group, creating a list of artifacts that would represent the group. Finding a common starting point can be difficult, so I suggest that each group examine the members' artifacts and look for some common themes. When they have completed their lists, I have them rank the artifacts and annotate the list. Finally, I have each group give an oral presentation of their lists and discuss the common and diverse cultural themes that exist within the classroom.

> *On the broadest level, the overall objective of the link is to expose students to physical and human cultures that are different from their own.*

Establishing Links

Establishing links may take time. It may be weeks before you receive a response to the letters that you send to other schools. Establishing the links with other teachers during the summer or year before can be more efficient, but having students take part in the linking process can be an important lesson in group decision making as well as in geography.

On the broadest level, the overall objective of the link is to expose students to physical and human cultures that are different from their own. If you are in a rural school, you might wish to link with an urban school. You might wish to look for schools in communities where families have a different socioeconomic background from that of your students. Census Bureau reports will help you and your students. The reports can provide information on the average income of an area as well as its population. It is important to target schools based on your own objectives for students.

What Addresses Do You Need?

Your objective is to get the name and address of a school that you think will work best for you. Your goal is to find a school and teacher willing to work with you. For my classes, the common link already exists: both communities are on the Mississippi. You will have your own link. The culture of the kids in the school you want to link with should be different from yours.

If you are looking for a school in a small town, write to the local postmaster or postmistress. That person might send you the addresses of the schools or school district offices in town (in many cases there may be only one school) or forward your letter to an appropriate school. For larger towns and cities, your search may be a little more difficult. Many local libraries have phone books of other cities from which you can get the addresses you need. If you cannot get the addresses from the phone books, long-distance information will also give you the addresses you need.

Your search for possible schools could also begin with letters to the office of the superintendent of a school district. Someone there will be able to send you the names and addresses of all the schools in the district. Also request the names of principals and department chairs. A letter to the chair of the department you wish to link with gets you closer to the source. You could also write to the city office of tourism. You can request maps of the city. You can use the maps, along with census data, to target the school you wish to link with.

There are undoubtedly other ways to find a partner school. There is no rigid formula for establishing links. Finding a school to link with can be a good problem-solving exercise for you and your students. Encourage students to be creative and to explore as many alternatives as possible. Perhaps you would like to link with a teacher you know or met at a conference. Be creative and let us know how you established your links.

Once you have written to a specific school, make a follow-up call. This call can secure a link between you and another teacher. Securing such a link is important because, in a sense, you will be team teaching with any teacher you link with. You and that teacher will need to find ways to plan and coordinate your activities.

Now the fun begins! Think simply! That is the motto for the first exchange projects. One of the best ways to keep it simple is to make it personal. A good place to start is with an exchange of artifacts, using the introductory artifact collection presented earlier as a model.

Creating a Culture Box

A culture box is a collection of artifacts that represent your culture (for a more complete description of culture boxes, see chapter 9, by Hilary Stock). Spend a class period brainstorming with your students about the artifacts you would like to send. I bring the box into class so that students can see the size with which they have to work. I also set a limit on the number of artifacts that we will send. Let students name as many artifacts as possible, then have the students rank the artifacts based on the ones that will tell another culture the most about the students. You may wish to have your students do the ranking in small groups and then present those rankings to the whole class.

Once we have decided on a list of artifacts and students volunteer to collect them, I try to spread out the duties so that all students are involved. If need be, I will pair students. I also give them strict deadlines for collecting artifacts. Before sending the box, the students create an annotated list of artifacts and take pictures for our records.

The following is a partial list of artifacts collected by ninth graders for an exchange with a group of students in Sudan:

- *Twin Cities* magazine
- napkins, with logo, from their favorite hangout
- a Hostess Twinkee
- a pine cone
- a local TV guide
- a T-shirt with their school logo on it
- a map of the city with their school and other important places marked

- a tape of the students' favorite music
- a bag of wild rice with recipes
- photographs of the students involved

You will also need to collect money in order to mail your boxes back and forth. It will not cost much ($5 to $10 for a five-pound box), and your school or department may very well pay the cost. But if you and your students contribute to a mailing fund it will increase the sense of proprietorship and pride they have in the project.

Receiving a Culture Box

When you receive the culture box from your partner school, spend some time discussing the similarities and differences between the two groups. Focus on the significance of individual artifacts. Take this opportunity to discuss the way one cultural group interprets another. For example, students in a farm community might send a small planting tool to students in the inner city. To the students in the city, the tool may mean a backward way of life, but to the students from the farming community it means something completely different.

To involve the rest of your school in the project, set up a display table in the library and hang any maps and pictures you have received. Last year I hung the map of Sudan as well as the pictures we received on the bulletin board in my room. Students who weren't involved in the project became interested and began following our progress.

The River Culture

Cultural box exchanges are also an excellent way of getting students to discover more about the Mississippi River or other geographical regions. Your culture box (or second culture box) could contain artifacts found along the river or artifacts about the river. Students could collect soil samples, rocks, items left by humans along the river, and sketches or photographs of trees, buildings, or boats that travel the river. Included in this box could be folktales, stories, and yarns about the river. This activity can help students understand the importance of the river to their broader community as well as to the community of your partner school. Students can compare the differences of the artifacts found in the two places and discuss how those differences are related to the geography of each place.

Other activities that explore the river culture in your area will help students understand how culture is determined not only by place but also by time. For example, there are literally hundreds of ancient Native American temple mounds along the river. The mounds and other artifacts provide clues to the way many native cultures lived before Europeans arrived and how those cultures changed after Europeans arrived.

Creating a Book on Native American History in Your Area

The production of books is no longer the exclusive right of monks in monasteries or large publishing houses in New York. Today, a group of students with access to computers, the right programs, and a copy machine can produce a professional-looking book with charts, maps, and illustrations.

What can students learn by producing a book on the history of a Native American group in your area? First, students will be able to see and understand the cultural changes, both subtle and revolutionary, that occur over time. Second, students will be able to understand that each Native American group has their own, unique "Native American culture." Producing a book is also a way to encourage artistic and creative thinking skills in students who excel in more traditional forms of academics and in students who may be more successful learning in this way. You can also accomplish numerous skill objectives with this project. Students will be able to improve writing, research, and organization skills as well as skills in visual arts, design, and layout.

You can set up the project by devising an organizational scheme. Students can form groups based on the organizational method you choose. There are several schemes to consider.

. . . culture is determined not only by place but also by time.

You may wish to organize your book by themes: technology, religion, village life, agriculture and hunting, traditions and customs. Or you may wish to organize by historical periods.

Within the groups each student can be assigned to take responsibility for a particular phase of the production:

- research
- writing (text organization)
- illustrations and maps
- computer layout

Assigning responsibilities does not mean that one student does all the writing or research. It merely means that she or he is responsible for overseeing that phase of the project.

Encourage students to use nontraditional as well as traditional forms of research. School, public, and college or university libraries can provide a great deal of information. But of equal value will be interviews with local Native Americans who know and understand the history and culture of their people. Your students or you can contact historical societies, reservations (contact reservation schools!), or nearby universities or colleges to find Native Americans who are interested in being interviewed. If possible, have them come in and talk to your whole class as well as having an individual or pair of students interview them.

When students interview someone, I stress the need for preparation and practice. They should devise specific as well as general questions. I have students practice the interview with other students to help the interviewers feel relaxed and confident during the actual interview. Finally, I have students tape the interview, as doing so will reinforce the need for accuracy.

When students have completed their research and developed an organization scheme, they can word process, edit, and devise a layout

Encourage students to use nontraditional as well as traditional forms of research.

for the material on a computer. You may wish to have students come up with a name for their publishing company. With a good copy machine, you can print as many copies of the book as you need. You and your students can choose any method of binding based upon the amount of money you have to spend. A book produced with materials found in school can cost little or no money. Various forms of binding exist, from staple and pressure binds to three-ring binders. For more professional bindings consult a local printer. Having students do all the work can build their confidence and be a great source of pride.

Once you and your link partner have completed books, exchange copies. You can then begin to compare the two Native American groups. You can focus on the specific cultural differences between the groups as well as the similarities. Have students explore the relationship between the geographic places and the specific aspects of the cultures that flourished there.

You can create books on any topics that you and your link partner choose. Other topics could include technology on the river (attempts by humans to control the river/nature), steamboats, the history of African Americans' experience with the river, and ecosystems of the river. The list is endless. Write us about the project that you choose.

Cooperative Projects

The activities described above have focused on exchanges. You can also base activities on cooperation and joint decision making. The goal of such projects is for students to make decisions and work cooperatively with students from other cultures.

When we talk about a small world we are also talking about more and more people being affected by problems in one region of the world. For example, depletion of natural resources such as the rain forest in Brazil and Indonesia has caused problems that have global consequences. To solve these problems, people from many cultures must participate in the decision-making process. To accomplish such cooperation, we must fortify our students with a new attitude that promotes working with people from other cultures to solve problems.

Cleaning the River

A few years ago I took a group of students to a stretch of the Mississippi River south of downtown Minneapolis. We were going to sketch and photograph flowers and other plants that grow wild there. It is about a seventy-foot vertical drop from the road to the shoreline. As we walked down the path we started to pick up soda can rings, soda and beer cans, paper, and other trash. In the next hour we collected six garbage bags of trash. I was impressed with the way my students initiated our impromptu clean-up. It was one of the students who suggested that we go to a store and buy trash bags and spend the afternoon cleaning an area of the river instead of just photographing plants.

. . . we must fortify our students with a new attitude that promotes working with people from other cultures to solve problems.

The river clean-up project is designed to get students involved in the link to clean up their stretch of the river, reach out to the greater community to become involved, and propose some long-term solutions for keeping the banks of the river free from trash.

To begin the project, take students on a field trip to the river. Coordinate this trip with your link partner. Photograph the area before you collect the trash as well as when you have finished. Have students collect trash for about one-half hour. Then have students create a list of specific items of trash left behind by humans. Discuss with your students effective ways to clean up the river and prevent further abuse. Focus on what they can do in their community. You can also use the opportunity to discuss the items of trash as artifacts of our society. Have a few members of the class take notes on your discussion.

Exchange the notes and photographs with your link partner. When you receive your partner's notes and photographs, compare the ideas with yours. As a class, devise several courses of action that you can take and exchange them with your partner. Stress with your students that whatever project they choose, they must agree and coordinate with their link partner.

When decisions must be made in an exchange, look for expedient ways to communicate with your link partner. One way is for each group to choose a representative who will communicate by phone. Another way is to use a FAX machine. If your school does not have one, try to find a parent or local business person who does—someone who would like to be involved in the project.

One project that classes can do together is to sponsor a river clean-up day in each community. Both classes must agree on the day. Have students begin by working on an advertising campaign. Here are some ideas:

• Work with your art teacher and have students create posters that they can display at school, in malls, and in businesses in the community. If each student makes two copies of her or his poster, one set can go to your link school.

• Create a pamphlet of student ideas on how the community can keep the river clean and pass it out with the announcement for the clean-up day. Exchange the ideas with your link partner so that one pamphlet can be created to serve both communities. The pamphlet can be laid out on a computer and photocopied. Enlist the help of local businesses to distribute the pamphlets and announcements.

• Have students create an advertisement for local radio stations. You can divide the tape into two 30-second segments so that you and your link partner can both contribute to the tape. Have your students contact local radio stations and ask them to play the spot as a public service.

Try other cooperative service projects. The students might take water samples and test them for quality. Students could then research the types of products causing pollution in the river and print and distribute that research in the community.

Students could also measure erosion of the river's banks and the effects that human intervention has had on erosion. Students could spend a Saturday counting boats on the river and categorizing the types of boats. Students could then meet with community leaders and discuss solutions to erosion and other problems. Your students will be able to see the connection between the different uses of the river and amount of erosion.

What Will Students Learn from Link Projects?

Here is a partial list of what I have found students gain from the Mississippi link or a similar link:

• They will understand and define culture in a way that is relevant to them.

• They will understand and analyze the geographic relationship between a place and the culture of the people who occupy that place.

• They will understand what a cultural artifact is and why it is important to know what artifacts tell us about a culture as well as the limitations of what artifacts can convey.

• They will rate various artifacts based on the perceived importance of the artifacts to the culture at a particular time.

• They will understand how one's culture influences the decisions one makes. Students can experience cultural influences on all levels from personal decisions (such as marriage and money management) to group decisions that involve laws and the selection of leaders.

• They will understand that culture changes over time.

• They will evaluate the ways in which cultures change. Some aspects of our culture change at revolutionary speed, yet other aspects of our culture change in subtle ways over long periods of time.

• They will develop fair criteria to evaluate cultures. We tend to evaluate other cultures based on the goals and accomplishments of our own culture. By developing fair criteria I mean that students should evaluate a culture based on a particular culture's goals, perceived needs, and philosophy.

• They will make decisions about individual cultures based on multicultural understanding. As our world gets smaller, new problems arise between people of different cultures. In our classrooms, schools, and communities we see many cultures operating at once. Problems and friction develop because our decisions and actions, which affect others, are based on our cultural perspective. To avoid conflict on local and global levels, students must learn to take a multicultural approach to problem solving.

• They will work toward solutions to problems with people from other cultures.

More Projects and Ideas

The following projects can be either direct exchanges or cooperative ventures:

• Video letters. (For detailed information on this activity, see chapter 4, by Larry Johnson.) Video letters can focus on your school, community or town, or more specific aspects of your culture. For example, a school in St. Paul may want to do a video letter on the importance of shipping to the local economy. You can do cooperative projects with video letters as well. Agree on a subject that both groups would like to pursue. Have one group film the first segment of the video letter and send it to their link partner, who can then complete the project.

• Fund-raising campaigns. Have the two link groups choose an organization or cause to raise money for throughout the year. One method includes having students collect only pennies. One first-grade class in Minneapolis collected $98 in pennies in three weeks. The students can solicit pennies from family, friends, and neighbors. A campaign run over the course of months can net a good deal of money.

• Cooperative books. Using the principles described earlier on writing a book on Native American history, two linked classrooms can create one book. Once the linked classes agree on a subject, teachers can spread the assignments out between the two classes.

• Stories and folktales. Stories, legends, and folktales have always been part of the cultures that grew along the river. Have your students collect stories that are specific to your area. Print and exchange them with your link partner.

Expanding Your Links:
Including More Cultures

The links do not have to end after one year and they need not be limited to two classes. Most middle and junior high school teachers have up to five separate classes. One method of branching out is to have each class link with a class from a

The more your links expand, the more your students will learn about themselves as well as specific cultures.

different community along the river. As your projects develop over the course of the year you can integrate your linked classes. Classes can share the information and artifacts that are being exchanged.

Another method for expanding links is for you and your link partner to choose another community with which to link. Information and activities can then go through four schools. To keep expanding, have each school choose another school with which to link. The process is time consuming but rewarding. The more your links expand, the more your students will learn about themselves as well as specific cultures. Teachers working cooperatively in a school can continue these links into a second and even a third year.

Going International

As your links expand and students learn more about the diverse cultures within their own country, you may wish to broaden your links to expose students to more diverse cultures around the world. You need not give up the Mississippi model to do so. The focal point of your search can be schools located in communities that are on major river systems in other countries. For example, you may wish to connect with other students by looking for communities on the Yangtze River in China, the Amazon River in Brazil, or the Congo River in Zaire.

To find schools in different countries, begin by contacting the country's embassy in Washington, D.C. (see Appendix B). You can also use parents who have traveled, worked, or conducted business overseas, or who are immigrants from another country. Let me emphasize again that the process of establishing a link can take time, but the rewards are enormous.

Finally, there is a large international school network around the world. Our link in Sudan was with an international school in Khartoum. Several projects throughout the year provided truly insightful experiences for both groups of students. Addresses for international school organizations as well as for embassies are in Appendixes A and B.

Conclusion

Linking along the Mississippi River is just one model for establishing links. It provides tremendous potential for students to learn about their own as well as other cultures. I have found in my experience with links that as your ties with another group grow, students become more motivated. They meet deadlines for finishing and mailing projects with greater ease and eventually become the propelling force behind the link.

You can apply the tools students develop through an in-depth link with one culture to the study of other cultures. The lessons born of active involvement in the linking projects will stick with students far longer than lessons learned by traditional methods.

If you decide to conduct a link, whether it be intrastate, intranational, or international, write to us at the address below and explain your link. We would like to collect addresses of teachers and schools interested in linking so that we might facilitate more links in the years ahead.

Walter Enloe and Ken Simon
c/o Institute of International Studies
214 Social Sciences Building
267 19th Avenue South
Minneapolis, MN 55455

or

Walter Enloe and Ken Simon
c/o Zephyr Press
P.O. Box 13448
Tucson, AZ 85732-3448

Eventually, all things merge into one, and a river runs through it. The river was cut by the world's great flood and runs over rocks from the basement of time. On some of the rocks are timeless raindrops.

—Norman Maclean, *A River Runs through It*

4

VIDEO LETTER EXCHANGES

by Larry Johnson

*This instrument can teach, it can illuminate; yes, and it can
even inspire. But it can do so only to the extent that humans
are determined to use it to those ends.*

—Edward R. Murrow

I've been a storyteller since the late 1960s when I worked my way
through broadcast school at the University of Minnesota, directing
summer camps, telling tales, and helping young people make primi-
tive TV programs with the new portable reel-to-reel equipment that
had just come out. I began in the university program in international
broadcasting but couldn't see how to bring that experience to young
people. So I switched to a regular educational TV sequence and began
to explore how to make video more participatory for children—to
make it function like a storyteller, connecting live and personally
with the audience. About 1986, when I'd long since quit trying to
think about international broadcasting, I found myself, thanks to
principal Mary Schepman, working half-time at Longfellow International Elementary School. My job? Teaching young people to tell
stories and to make video letters to exchange with other, often international, schools.

As has happened with a number of people exploring the potential of portable video, I stumbled into this idea. Shortly after I helped establish a participatory TV channel at Minneapolis Children's Health Center, friends of a boy dying of leukemia asked if they could make a video for him because they weren't allowed to enter his isolation room to visit. We helped them make and play the tape over the hospital closed-circuit channel, but we also let the friends stand before the live camera so their patient friend could see them as they cheered him up in person over the call-in TV telephone. Despite the sadness of the overall situation, it was a joyous, meaningful day, and it demonstrated the power of using TV to allow personalized visiting when it wasn't otherwise possible.

During that time we didn't call it video letter exchange, but it's really what we got ourselves into. When patients from nearby schools were hospitalized for a long time, often in isolation, we helped or asked classmates to make a video of themselves and their current activities to share with their absent friend. Sometimes these patients even returned videos from the hospital to the school, maintaining personal connections.

In 1982, I became cable coordinator for the Minneapolis school district, but I remained interested primarily in these kinds of personalized, two-way, student-made video exchanges. In 1984 I met Ben Selisker, who had come from Pennsylvania, where this kind of video exchange had begun between language students at Temple University and native speakers in other countries. The idea had then spread to the public schools in Philadelphia, and some of us became interested in a similar exchange here.

> *That's what a video letter exchange is: a way for ordinary people . . . to bring light to the world by visiting and getting to know each other better on video when it's not possible to travel to each other's places.*

Shortly after that, Roger Wangen of the State Department of Education arranged for me to do some workshops for teachers, showing them how to do this kind of international video exchange. The night before the workshops, I had a dream in which I was preparing for a workshop. Over and over I went down the list: "Portapaks, tapes, paper, pencil, clay pots? . . ." My list kept stopping on "clay pots," and of course, when I woke up, everything made sense but that.

I described the dream to my wife, Elaine Wynne, who is also a storyteller trained deeply in folklore, and she said, "Of course, spider grandmother brought light to the world using clay pots." And that's it! That's what a video letter exchange is: a way for ordinary people, even children, to bring light to the world by visiting and getting to know each other better on video when it's not possible to travel to each other's places.

Video Letters as International Understanding

One of the people in that workshop, Kate Murray of Children's Museum, secured a small grant for Elaine and me to work with Longfellow Elementary in St. Paul. The school wanted to exchange a video with a British school during the 1985 British Festival in the Twin Cities. We made the tape, and then as has often happened, we found we were having difficulty finding our school contact in England. Elaine and I were going to Germany that fall to participate in the two hundredth anniversary of the Grimm's Fairy Tale Collection, so we arranged to take the St. Paul video with us and find a British school on our own time. (As many of you know, if you can make something new happen once, it's usually easier the next time.)

When we got to London, we stayed a few days with Sondra Pollerman, a storyteller and clown, who was helping us find a school to exchange with. When she actually saw the tape, she said, "Oh, that's what it is. I'm clowning at a school tomorrow. I know I can get them to watch this and let you come in and make a tape with them." Then I realized something I've seen so many times since: Those of us who have grown up with expensive commercial TV can't conceive of a personally made video until we've seen it. In other words, Sondra

63

and the schools didn't think they could make a video because they didn't think they could make what they'd been watching at home, but that isn't what video exchange is.

The next morning Sondra showed the tape at Furzedown Primary and the kids made a plan. That afternoon Elaine and I helped them make a response video, and the students in St. Paul loved it, even though they couldn't believe "rap and break dancing had already gotten to London."

Late the next summer, Maythee Kanar of Metro State University gave us the entry form for the Tokyo Video Festival, pointing out that the special category this year was called "Video Letter Exchange." The deadline was three days away, and I was busy so I thought of not entering. I'd heard plenty of people downgrade video letters because when elementary children really make it themselves (as opposed to participating in the production, with adults doing much of the technical work and imposing their standards), it "doesn't look professional." However, I thought, "I need a composite tape for workshops," so I took a few hours and put pieces of both "letters" together, showing what was sent together with the response.

The tape went into the competition, just barely in time, and about November 6 we got a phone call saying, "You have won the grand prize in the Tokyo Video Festival. Can somebody be here November 16 to accept the prize?" For the first time ever, a tape in the special category (aimed at innovative uses as opposed to "slicker, professional" video) won grand prize, and since that time JVC has kept the video letter exchange category and continues to promote this valuable use of portable video.

Beginning Lessons

One of the first things young people learn when they make video is that TV (though it carries the message of "quick and easy" to the ultimate) is not easy to make. It takes a lot of working together, planning, reading, and writing, even to make a simple student video letter. Certainly student videomakers should be allowed freedom to create and to express, and of course some of them, like some adults, will go for the quick, cheap laugh and popularity. But I believe a teacher's job in this project is to direct students to show and tell ideas that aren't commonly seen on commercial TV—to give students at least a strong suggestion of what TV *isn't* doing so that some or even many of them will be persuaded not to copy popular, commercial TV when they make their own. Our job is to give them a sense of wanting to "tell the stories," show the scenes, advertise the products that TV often forgets.

I don't believe in censorship, but I do believe that everyone who puts out information has a responsibility to the audience, and I believe in teaching that responsibility to young videomakers, whether they'll grow up to work in TV or just to be home consumers of it.

The What, Who, Where, Why, and How

When I was in broadcasting school and we had to learn to *write* a news story for print or broadcast, we were taught to look for and answer these questions. You can also use them when making videos.

What is a video letter exchange? It's an inexpensive, two-way visit to another place when you can't go in person and when writing won't do. (For example, how do you use words to describe snow and cold to a person in Uganda who has never experienced it? Children on a video letter decided to show a blizzard, snow houses, and how they put on warm clothes.) It's done home-video style, with portable video equipment, and can allow ongoing visits between schools, families, hospitals, and other organizations or groups.

Whom do you trade videos with? For starters and practice, one class might trade with another class in your own school. After that, a lot has to do with what you hope to learn from another place. I am personally interested in trades with schools or groups showing young people telling stories or growing children's gardens. Social studies or language classes might wish to trade with a group in a country being studied or one speaking the language being learned. Hearing-impaired students may prefer ongoing exchanges in sign language (a natural for video), and students who have a long-term hospitalized classmate might engineer a video visit with their friend.

The ideas are limitless if you merely think, "Where do we want to go that we cannot physically go?" Indeed, you might want to organize video letters into the curriculum and plan to have students trade with students in other grades who are studying the same subject. Or you might want to set up some progressive pattern, such as first graders trade with other classes in your school, second graders with another school in the district, third graders with a school elsewhere in the state, fourth graders with a school in a nearby state, fifth graders with a school somewhere in the U.S., and sixth graders with an international school (and, of course, I'm assuming that secondary students might start immediately at some higher level).

What do I need to make a video letter exchange? All you need is (1) a blank tape, (2) a portable video system such as a camcorder, and (3) a person with some homestyle-video experience to help your students make their video. Of course, you also need a willing group or class to view your tape and respond in kind.

Who should do the taping? Someone who has access to equipment and knows how to operate it—teacher, parent, media specialist, cable access volunteer, video artist in residence, broadcast or video intern from the university, or a group of your students. I think involving only students, with only supervising adults, is the ideal, if you're willing or able to take the time and the relative chaos. Of course, the students who are taping need to work in smaller groups of about six with one of the above-mentioned adults, and I believe that adult should not be too locked in to creating a "professional-looking" (by adult broadcast standards) product. Also, the slicker the tape looks, the more likely you are to intimidate the group on the other end into not responding because they can't "compete." A video exchange between students should be likened to a neat, handwritten, loving note to a friend. Certainly you don't want a totally sloppy video that can't be seen or heard, but if the children do their best and you can see or hear a

You can make a fairly simple but very adequate video letter in just three class sessions.

message, you don't need Hollywood-style video. It's for the group you're exchanging with, not for a national, network-TV, channel-flipping audience.

How do I do make a video letter in a regular classroom? There are several ways, depending on your time, teaching style, the age of your students, and general preferences. You can make a fairly simple but very adequate video letter in just three class sessions: one to plan with your students what should be on the tape; one for an adult or older student who is very competent with the equipment to tape the "scenes" systematically and in order; and one to view the video you get in response. If your scheduling and style allow for small groups of students to work cooperatively, you can make a bigger project of it with students doing all the taping, not necessarily in order. Students can edit the video later to make a good product.

What does a video letter look like? The planning outline I work with takes under twenty minutes. (Shorter is okay, and fifteen might be better, especially if you have to convert the tape. The price of conversion goes up after fifteen minutes.) You should introduce yourselves, show what you have decided to show about your school or community, and ask some questions you'd like your partner school to respond to. Of course, at the beginning, fade up from black and then fade to black at the end.

The introductions can be as simple as students standing before the camera and talking about themselves. (Despite all the bad press about "talking heads," network TV is full of them—it's just they've been identified as "stars," and in your video letter the students are stars.) However, I wouldn't use individual introductions if the group is bigger than one class. If the video is coming from the whole school, maybe everyone should stand out front and wave, or show the school and then where you are on the map. Get the students to use their imaginations to create an informative, fun introduction. What you choose to show the other school is wide open, but it means thinking about taping plays, events, interviews, and so forth, and making the necessary arrangements to get them done. I've seen a Pueblo school in New Mexico show the kimonos they all made while studying

Japan, and I've made a video with students showing a tour of their little Wisconsin town preparing to build a landing strip for UFOs. From Japan we got a scene of a beach game with blindfolded students trying to break a watermelon, and our Spanish-speaking students said, "That's like when we break piñatas at fiesta"—so that's what they sent back.

What kinds of questions should we ask? Try to use visual questions. Don't ask, "Do you like your school?" Rather, ask, "Could you show us the things you like best about your school?" I said it's okay for students merely to stand before the camera and talk when introducing themselves, but after that you want to use the video to show things in their environment. Visual questions lead the other school to a visual response, rather than to putting someone in front of the camera again to say yes or no. It's a good exercise as part of your planning to brainstorm and create visual questions to direct the other school to show you what you're curious about. Here's part of a list of questions generated by Ramsey students for a video exchange with New Mexico:

- If you ride buses to school, would you show us what they look like?
- Could we see what the neighborhood around your school is like?
- Please show us the musical instruments you play and what they sound like.
- Would you show us what foods you eat at school lunch?
- Could you show us how to play your favorite games?
- Would you show us how you solve some school problems?

Of course, showing some of these things on your tape might elicit a response in kind automatically, but not always. You will be more certain of getting the response you want, for example, if you show the neighborhood around your school and then ask to see theirs.

What about language differences? Even if it's not the main focus of your learning and the reason for the exchange, learning a little of another language can always be valuable. Obviously if you get a tape all in Japanese and you weren't counting on it, you've got a bit of a problem, but don't let that happen. Find someone who knows the native language of the country you're exchanging with and send some of your tape in that language—maybe the "hellos," a song, and a story. Then ask the partner school to do the same. When we exchanged with Japan, I aligned the project with Sallie Sudo's class, because she is originally from Japan. She taught her students some Japanese to send and translated what came back. Had she not been at the school when the opportunity to trade with Japan came up I think we would have gone for help to Washburn High, where some students learn Japanese. Many people would like the opportunity to refine their language skills further and to help in international education.

How do we find a place to exchange with? One of the best ways is mentioning it in conversation or at a meeting and making the acquaintance of a willing person in another state or country. We traded with Indonesia because I met a teacher from there at the National Storytelling Congress. My stepson, Dan Wynne, just left to teach in Ecuador, so we will finally be able to exchange with a Spanish-speaking school. He's already worked with and is excited about the idea of video exchange. I've started exchanging videos with schools growing gardens because I mentioned it at the 1989 National Children's Garden Symposium.

What about tape conversions? A VHS tape going anywhere in the U.S. will play fine in a VHS machine (most home or portable school video now is VHS rather than BETA), but make sure the school you're sending to has VHS (if that's what you use) not 3/4" or BETA.

A VHS tape going to Japan and some other international sites also plays fine, but put your VHS tape in a British VHS machine, and you get nothing intelligible. Don't ask me to explain why—just accept the fact that it needs to be converted. However, international sites with the same VHS format as the U.S. (thus not requiring conversion) include the Bahamas, Barbados, Bolivia, Canada, Chile, Columbia, Costa Rica, Cuba, Curaçao, Dominican Republic, Ecuador, El Salvador,

Guam, Guatemala, Hawaii, Honduras, Japan, Korea, Mexico, Panama, Peru, Philippines, Puerto Rico, Samoa, Suriname, Taiwan, Trinidad, Venezuela, and the Virgin Islands.

When and how should we send out video letters? If you're doing just one exchange and wanting it to happen with "this year's class," allow plenty of time to get a return by the end of the school year. If it's to be an ongoing exchange over several years, which is usually preferable, the timing may not be so important.

Sending the tapes book rate in a padded tape mailer is a good way to mail, but if you're sending overseas, you might want to ask about actual delivery time and spend a little more for a faster rate. If a parent or someone connected to the school is traveling to where your tape is going, you might ask that person to carry the video. The personal touch might be nice, and in fact sometimes successful exchanges are made by a person carrying a tape over and then helping the school to view and make a return video.

Technical Tips

I realize I've emphasized that you should not be concerned with duplicating the "professionalism" or "slickness" of commercial video when you exchange video letters, but quality is certainly good to strive for. Indeed, the more you work with video, the better you'll get, so here are some ideas to make your video letters look better:

• If you want, you can make titles and credits with some computer programs or in-camera with most of the newer models. However, these features are not necessary. You can also make titles and credits by drawing on sidewalk, blackboard, or paper (a 3"-x-4" rectangle is best), or by using an existing sign (for example, your school's name on the side of the building). Also, a perfectly acceptable video letter opening is to fade up from black to a student saying "Hi, . . ." and then you can close by saying good-bye and fading again to black.

• Practice zoom and focus before you start shooting, but don't plan to use a lot of zoom in or zoom out while you're recording. Use it to set up close-ups or wider shots before you record them on your tape. If you want viewers to see something well, as if they were sitting right by it, use the close-up and a tripod for a more stable shot, and hold the shot long enough so viewers can comprehend it. The power of good video (even school-made video) is that everyone watching can see a tiny object as if she or he were the only one sitting in front of it.

• If possible, use an earpiece plugged into your camera to monitor audio while you record, or at least check that the audio level needle is jumping so you don't spend a lot of time taping only to find no sound on the tape. Audio should be clear and easy to hear. The camera's internal microphone does a good job of picking up group singing or other general sound, but whenever possible, individuals should use a hand-held mike plugged directly into the recording deck. Have the speaker hold the mike near her or his mouth. Speakers should also avoid scratching or rolling the mike between their hands. Even in person, someone who mumbles is not communicating. Students should speak distinctly, not too softly, and not until they've been signaled that the tape is actually rolling.

If you plan to use music, avoid popular, copyrighted music unless it's a case of students demonstrating what music they like. Aside from copyright issues, this project is creative, and students should be encouraged to share something they've done themselves.

• Color cameras need to be white-balanced, or if they're new, set on automatic white-balanced (read your instruction manual). Also, don't allow cameras to be pointed into the sun, bright lights, or out the window from indoors. Doing so can damage your camera, or at least ruin the picture you're trying to take.

• Finally, power. If you're shooting indoors, check on extension cords and outlets before it's time to start. If you are outdoors, make sure your battery, or better yet, batteries, are charged, and don't count on a portable battery to give you more than twenty to thirty minutes of actual recording time.

After the First Tape, Then What?

Here's an area that more of us can write about in a few years, after we've had many ongoing exchanges. One idea is to get into "more elaborate video." What follows is the narrative and the video script version of "The Purse Snatcher," written by Patty Bomash's Chapter One students at Longfellow in 1988. It started when I showed them a video letter from Madison, Wisconsin, with a boy telling a detective story. The kids then wrote their own detective tale; I taught them to tell it and recorded an audiocassette for each of them. Then we rewrote the tale as video and shot it like a movie, scene by scene. Then we sent it back to Madison via video letter.

PURSE SNATCHERS

a story using *ch-* and *-ch* words
rooms 114, 120, and 122

It was the middle of the morning on the first day of the month. An old lady with gray hair, walking cane, and thick bifocal glasses was walking on the boardwalk next to the beach. She had her purse in her hand. She crossed the street and went into the bank to cash her Social Security check. When she came out of the bank, she walked toward the secondhand store and the deli. To get to the secondhand store, she had to walk past a large city church. Two teenagers were lounging on the steps in front of the church, apparently waiting for a bus.

As the old lady hobbled by, one of the kids said goodbye to her friend and walked down the steps. She elbowed the old lady, knocking her down. At this moment, the boy ran down the steps and snatched the old lady's purse.

Then a man who had been sitting in his car reading a newspaper jumped out and began chasing the kids. A woman ran out of the church and ran after the girl. The woman shouted, "Stop! Police! You're under arrest!"

In a short time the policeman and policewoman had the two kids under control. Then they helped the old lady get up. A squad car came to pick up the purse snatchers. The policeman and policewoman drove the old lady to the station to press charges against the kids.

Late that afternoon, three people were in the lunchroom at the police station having coffee together. One was the man from the car, one was the woman from inside the church, and one was the old woman. Now the old woman looked different. There was no cane and there were no thick bifocals. She looked a lot less helpless. The three were laughing and talking over their coffee.

"Well, Charity," the man said to the old lady, "we certainly caught those two purse snatchers this morning."

"Yes, Charlie. Let's hope that puts an end to the purse snatching in that neighborhood. Those kids have robbed a lot of old ladies in the last two months," said the old lady. "Let's finish our reports and wrap up the day. I've got to get home and cook a birthday dinner for my grandson. They're coming over tonight."

The three stood up, took their dishes to the counter, and left the lunchroom.

Here is the video version (each number represents a different scene).

VIDEO	AUDIO
1. "The Purse Snatchers" (written on blackboard)	Music
2. Hand crossing off last day of month on calendar	
3. Old lady with cane and bifocals walking down sidewalk and across street	
4. Shot of bank	
5. Banker	
6. Close-up of old lady	Lady: "I'd like to cash my Social Security check."
7. Old lady out door	

8. Old lady by church with
   two kids lounging
9. Man in car reading paper
10. Kids get up
11. One kid knocks old lady down
    and grabs purse
12. Purse snatcher runs
13. Man in car gets out and
    chases purse snatcher
14. Woman comes out of church
    door
15. Woman catches other kid
    who didn't take purse
16. Police car drives up
17. Man and woman help old
    woman up

18. Kids loaded in police car
19. Man, woman, and old woman
    having coffee; "old woman"
    removes wig

20. Close-up of old woman

Man in car: "Stop!
Police!"
Woman: "Stop!
You're under arrest!"

Man and woman:
"Well, I guess that
wraps that up."

Man: "Well, Charity,
we sure caught those
purse snatchers this
morning."
Old woman: "Yes,
Charlie. Let's hope that
ends the purse snatching
in this neighborhood.
Those kids have
robbed a lot of old
ladies in the last two
months. Let's finish our
reports and wrap it up.
I've got a birthday
dinner to cook for my
grandson."

21. All three bus dishes and
    screen fades to black
22. Credits—students' names

Helpful Books and Organizations

Children's Stories about TV

I collected the following list of children's tales about TV because I think storytellers and writers need to start knowing and telling more stories about TV, rather than continuing to let it tell us so many stories. However, since part of the intent of making video letters is to learn about TV, perhaps some of the stories about TV might be helpful supplements; next someone needs to write a story about children making video letters; and of course, don't forget the children's books on other countries and cultures. These stories would be good references for researching information about the country you wish to exchange with, as well as for formulating questions to ask them.

Angell, Judie. *A Word from Our Sponsor*. New York: Dell, 1979.

Alfred leads a consumer rebellion against TV advertising.

Berenstain, Stan, and Jan Berenstain. *The Berenstain Bears and Too Much TV*. New York: Random House, 1984.

Mama Bear decides no one will watch TV for one week.

Blume, Judy. *Tales of a Fourth Grade Nothing*. New York: EP Dutton, 1972.

Fudge seems the perfect boy for the Toddle-Bike commercial . . . until the filming.

Bond, Michael. *Paddington on Screen*. Boston: Houghton Mifflin, 1982.

Brown, Marc. "The Bionic Bunny Show." *Atlantic Monthly*, 1984.

The story shows how the stunts and effects are accomplished backstage on "Bionic Bunny."

Buchwald, Art. *Irving's Delight*. New York: David McKay, 1975.

A famous French detective is called in to rescue a beloved cat in this spoof of cat commercials.

Byars, Betsy. *The TV Kid*. New York: Viking, 1976.

Lennie imagines he's a TV hero until he has to live through real-life terror in an abandoned cottage.

Carris, Joan. *Witch-Cat*. Philadelphia: J B Lippincott, 1984.

A magic cat learns about the twentieth century by watching TV.

Cleary, Beverly. *Ramona and Her Father*. New York: William Morrow, 1977.

Ramona hopes to earn a million dollars doing TV commercials while her father is out of work.

———. *Ramona Quimby, Age 8*. New York: William Morrow, 1981.

Ramona gives her book report in the form of a commercial.

Cohen, Miriam. *Jim Meets the Thing*. New York: Greenwillow Books, 1981.

Jim feels badly about being the only first grader afraid of a TV monster until Jim rescues his friend from a real praying mantis.

Collier, James. *Rich and Famous: The Further Adventures of George Stable*. New York: Four Winds, 1975.

George sings and plays guitar on a TV pilot.

Gerson, Corrine. *Son for a Day*. New York: Atheneum, 1980.

Danny makes friends with divorced fathers and their sons at the zoo. Making friends with Ms. Anderson gets his story on television.

Harris, Mark. *Confessions of a Prime Time Kid*. New York: Lothrop, Lee and Shepard, 1985.

A thirteen-year-old TV star writes his memoirs.

Heide, Florence. *The Problem with Pulcifer*. Philadelphia: J B Lippincott, 1982.

Pulcifer's parents are worried because he refuses to watch TV.

Heide, Florence, and Roxanne Heide. *A Monster Is Coming, A Monster Is Coming*. New York: Franklin Watts, 1980.

Little brother encounters a monster sneaking in the window while his sister is totally absorbed in a TV show.

Heilbroner, Joan. *Tom and the TV Cat*. New York: Random House, 1984.

Tom the cat is a "watch-aholic."

Hicks, Clifford. *Alvin Fernald—TV Anchorman* Orlando, Fla.: Holt, Rinehart, and Winston, 1980.

Alvin takes a TV news spot and solves an eleven-year-old crime.

Johnson, Larry. Box 9907, Minneapolis, Minnesota, 55458.

A few tales such as "Garden Hose Cable TV," available as reprints for SASEs. Two TV stories, "The Devil and the Tree House" and "This Is a Films Production—Destruction of Pompeii" available for $8.95 plus $1.00 postage and handling on KEY OF SEE'S audiotape *Running Scared and Flying High*.

Levy, Elizabeth. *Something Queer Is Going On*. New York: Delacorte, 1973.

Jill's dog is used in a TV commercial.

McPhail, David. *Fix-It*. New York: EP Dutton, 1984.

Emma is upset one Saturday when the TV won't work, but while the repairman is coming, her parents help her discover books.

Miles, Betty. *The Secret Life of the Underwear Champ*. New York: Alfred A Knopf, 1981.

Larry is thrilled to be doing TV commercials till he learns he will appear in underwear.

Personal Experience

> Here's where a lot of great TV stories can come from: the child who accidentally discovers you can permanently distort the TV image like a fun house mirror by waving a magnet in front of it; the boyfriend who doesn't like to stand in the corner and hold the antenna to get good reception. What are your unusual or funny or serious experiences with television?

Rettic, Margaret. "Television in the Snow" in *The Silver Touch and Other Family Christmas Stories*. New York: William Morrow, 1978.

> Two children discover they can see TV programs in holes they make in the snow.

Rodgers, Mary. *A Billion for Boris*. New York: Harper & Row, 1974.

> An old TV set shows programs a day in advance.

Rosen, Winifred. *Ralph Proves the Pudding*. New York: Doubleday, 1972.

> Ralph makes a TV commercial even though he feels the dessert tastes like shoes.

Shyer, Marlene. *Adorable Sunday*. New York: Scribner's, 1983.

> The story of Sunday's career as a TV commercial performer.

Weber, Judith. *Lights, Camera, Cats*. New York: Lothrop, Lee and Shepard, 1978.

West, Dan. *The Day the TV Blew Up*. Niles, Ill.: Albert Whitman, 1988.

> Ralph's TV explodes, and he discovers the library.

Wilde, Oscar. "The Selfish Giant."

> I consider this a TV story because when I first read it, I thought, "I like it but I can't tell it." Then I saw the animated TV version and changed my mind. More and more students in my story-telling classes are telling stories they heard on TV. I think that's good.

Wildsmith, Brian. *Daisy.* New York: Pantheon, 1984.

Daisy, an inquisitive cow, becomes a TV performer.

Video Production Handbooks

The trouble with many of these fine books is that they go out of print almost right away, but they are around, and if you can find them, they're valuable aids to involving young people in video.

Coloroso, Barbara. *Media for Kids.* Denver: Love Publishing Company, 1982.

Fuller, Barry J., Steve Kanaba, and Janyce Kanaba. *Single Camera Video Production Handbook.* Englewood Cliffs, N.J.: Prentice-Hall, 1982.

Kaplan, Don. *Video in the Classroom: A Guide to Creative Television.* White Plains, N.Y.: Knowledge Industry Publications, 1982.

Norwood, Nancy, ed. *The Video Handbook.* Intermedia Arts, 425 Ontario St. S.E., Minneapolis, MN 55414.

Robinson, Richard. *The Video Primer.* New York: Putnam, 1981.

Organizations

Global Education Motivators Network (Gemnet)
Chestnut Hill College
Germantown and Northwestern Avenues
Chestnut Hill, PA 19118-2695
(215) 248-1150

Gemnet specializes in a package of electronic mail and on-line global education information for schools. They have inherited the international video letters work begun by Alan Soffin at Temple University. They are presently talking about taking Soffin's work over and continuing to develop it.

JVC Company of America
41 Slater Drive
Elmwood Park, NJ 07407

JVC is the distributor of portable video equipment (and of course other electronic equipment). They sponsor the Tokyo Video Festival and support international video exchanges.

Key of See Storytellers
2615 S. 6th St.
Minneapolis, MN 55454
(612) 333-0970

Larry Johnson and Elaine Wynne, besides holding storytelling performances and workshops, do workshops and residencies on all kinds of video letter exchanges.

National Federation of Local Cable Programmers
Box 27290
Washington, DC 20038-7290

This organization promotes cable access TV throughout the U.S. Through the cable access center closest to you, they might be helpful in providing video help or equipment, if you need it. Cable access is very different from city to city; get to know yours.

National Telemedia Council
120 East Wilson Street
Madison, WI 53703
(608) 257-7712

This organization has been promoting "critical viewing skills" and quality broadcasting since radio days. As a demonstration model for the connection between making TV and watching it intelligently, they sponsored the first "made by kids" cable TV access channel in Sun Prairie, Wisconsin.

UNICEF Information Center on Children's Cultures
331 East 38th Street
New York, NY 10016
(212) 686-5522

> I have listed UNICEF because I have from them a "nonrepro-
> ducible without permission" list of organizations that do
> written and people-to-people exchanges. We should begin
> asking UNICEF and other organizations about help with video
> exchange contacts.

Video Village Network
147 West 22nd Street
New York, NY 10011
(212) 255-2718

> An affiliate of Martha Stuart Communications, Inc., they train
> women in developing countries to use portable video to show
> how they deal with various problems and issues. The tapes are
> then traded or made available to other areas needing the infor-
> mation. I have had brief discussions with them and feel there
> are some emerging possibilities for exchange as more and more
> schoolchildren exchange videos internationally.

5

CROSS-CULTURAL EXCHANGES VIA GAMES

by J. Leon Boler

> *Children's games constitute the most admirable social
> institutions. The game of marbles, for instance, . . . contains an
> extremely complex system of rules, that is to say, a code of laws, a
> jurisprudence of its own. Only the psychologist, whose profession
> obliges him [or her] to become familiar with this instance of
> common law, and to get at the implicit morality underlying it, is
> in a position to estimate the extraordinary wealth of these rules by
> the difficulty he [or she] experiences in mastering their details.*
> —Jean Piaget, *The Moral Judgment of the Child*

The exercise of having students work in small, cooperative groups
to create games evolved out of a project that Walter Enloe, Dan Puls,
and I began about a year ago. We were working on participatory
education projects and came up with the idea of putting together a
game supply kit that teachers could purchase. The creating of games
requires that students utilize higher-level cognitive activities, including application, analysis, synthesis, and evaluation. Teachers and
students can also use the games they create to link with other students in their communities and in national and international communities in a natural, fun, and creative way.

The creating of games requires that students utilize higher-level cognitive activities.

Most educational topics could be enhanced by the addition of create-a-game assignments. For example, an ecology class could have a quarter-long assignment (for which students would use intermittent class time) to design games whose themes focus on various pollution problems. To complete the assignment the students would have to research the issues involved and creatively simulate interconnected variables. Similarly, a cooperative group of students whose objective is to create a game that shares information about their culture with another student group must focus on what aspects of culture they wish to share and then research those aspects.

The create-a-game format fits nicely into many different subject areas and is easy to implement. Following is the teacher's guide we developed as part of our package, adapted for this publication.

Students Create Games for Cross-Cultural Exchange

Following this section, you will find information and worksheet suggestions for student cooperative groups. Student handouts follow the same outline presented here, except the information that is directed only to the teacher does not appear on student handouts. Information to include on student handouts includes the statement of purpose, the explanations of group behavior and the related point system, the definition and assignment of group member roles, the questions about the cooperation versus competition exercise, the discussion of game types, the worksheet, the types of thinking, the materials and activities of each assigned role, and the writing of rules.

Statement of Purpose and Explanation of Activity

Each group, through the process of creating a game, will develop or enhance skills in the following areas: cooperation and compromise with peers, problem solving, creative thinking, research, planning (separating final goals into manageable objectives), and craft.

Divide the class into groups of three to four students. Explain that each group will be inventing a new board game. Give each group information and the worksheet. Discuss with the students the purpose of creating games for cross-cultural exchange—how will the creators benefit?

Explain that you expect certain courteous behavior, including participation during group meetings, cooperation with peers, respect of peers, and effort in working on objectives. Also explain how points for behavior will be awarded.

Expectations of Group Members and the Related Point System[1]

Group members will be graded in three areas:

• *Participation:* The group must divide project tasks evenly among its members. Students will be expected to participate in and out of class. Group members must also participate in giving feedback during class discussions and in testing and analyzing the games created by other groups.

• *Cooperation and effort:* All team members will lose points if the group does not complete all worksheets, journal assignments, and other homework assigned to the team. Team members must cooperate and compromise with other team members. Teams must assign tasks to each of its members in a way that gives all members the opportunity to contribute equally to the project. Team members who do not put forth enough effort will receive fewer points.

• *Behavior:* Team members are expected **to follow directions** and **to refrain from making negative comments** about other group members or their projects. Team members are, however, encouraged to give

---

1. The section on how you expect group members to behave and the related point system was necessary for our work with some groups of adolescents. It may not be necessary for the students with whom you are working.

constructive feedback. The difference between negative comments and constructive feedback is often in the words chosen and the tone of voice used.

Team members may score points each day as follows: *Participation*—maximum of 10; *Effort*—maximum of 10; *Behavior*—maximum of 10.

Five Basic Elements of Small Group Cooperative Learning[2]

Following is an introduction or a refresher on cooperative education techniques. A number of books and articles on the subject are available. One source for a catalog and workshop information is Cooperative Learning Center, Pattee Hall, University of Minnesota, Minneapolis, MN 55455.

• Cooperative learning requires *positive interdependence*. In order for a learning situation to be cooperative, students must perceive that they are positively interdependent with the other members of their group, that they "sink or swim" together. You can encourage this perception by setting mutual goals (goal interdependence); by dividing labor (task interdependence); by dividing materials, resources, or information among group members (resource interdependence); by assigning students roles (role interdependence); and by giving joint rewards (reward interdependence).

• Cooperative learning requires *face-to-face interaction* among students. Positive interdependence in and of itself is not magical. It is the interaction patterns and verbal interchange among students promoted by positive interdependence that affect education outcomes.

• Cooperative learning requires *individual accountability for mastering the assigned material*. The purpose of the learning situation is to maximize the achievement of each student. Determining what you expect each student to master is necessary so that students can support and assist each other.

2. Source: Johnson & Johnson, *Cooperation in the Classroom*. Goodlettsville, Tenn.: Interactive Books, 1:10.

• Cooperative learning requires that students *use interpersonal and small-group skills appropriately*. Socially unskilled students will not be successful if you place them in a learning group and tell them to cooperate. Students must be taught the social skills they need for collaboration and be motivated to use these skills.

• Cooperative learning requires that *students be given the time and procedures for analyzing* (1) how well their learning groups are functioning and (2) the extent to which students are employing their social skills to help all group members achieve and maintain effective working relationships within the group.

Define and Assign Group Member Roles

Divide students into groups of three or four. I recommend that each group be heterogeneous, including high-, medium-, and low-ability students. Heterogeneous groups enhance the group's sharing of ideas and responsibilities. Include task-oriented students in each cooperative group.

Assign each member of the group to one of the following roles, or have the group members decide which student will fill each role:

Facilitator directs group meetings, sets meeting agenda, focuses the group in developing and assigning project tasks, encourages group member participation.

Checker checks to make sure that all group members have expressed their opinions when making project decisions, that the group completes team homework and journal assignments on time, and that the group does not make decisions or design and build the game in a rushed or haphazard fashion.

Materials handler takes responsibility for project materials and equipment and for negotiating the transfer of material between groups.

Secretary keeps minutes of group meetings, notes who is assigned what tasks, and reads minutes from previous meeting.[3]

[3] If there are fewer than four members in a group, the facilitator should assume secretarial responsibilities.

Assign a name to each cooperative group, then record the positions of each group member.

Cooperation versus Competition: An Exercise

Now that the groups have been formed, you can conduct a good exercise to help the students think about the advantages of cooperative versus competitive group interaction by using Hershey's Kisses or some other treat. Have each student find a partner who is about the same size. Then have the pairs place their elbows on a table or the floor and join hands in an arm wrestling position. Tell them that each time their partners' wrists touch the table or floor they will earn one Hershey's Kiss. Ready, set, go. Stop. Repeat the instructions. Ready, set, go. Stop. Repeat the instructions. At some point one or more of the pairs will catch on that the way to earn the most Kisses is to take turns letting their partners win—the cooperative approach. Discuss this approach and tie it into the cooperative learning groups and their upcoming assignments, using the following questions:

• How did you feel at first about the idea of competing against your partner? Confident? Worried?

• Do you think—be honest—that if you could always beat your partner you would?

• Would you have any sympathy for your partner if you kept beating him or her?

• When you figured out that if you cooperated you and your partner would *both* win more candy, how did your feelings toward your partner change?

• Which of the skills listed under *purpose* did you use as part of this exercise?

• What lesson did you learn from this exercise that you can relate to your group's goal of making a game?

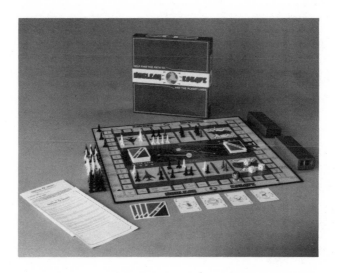

Discussion of Game Types

Discuss games in general. Some are focused on a theme in which players play a specific role. For example, in Monopoly, players become wheeler-dealers in real estate. Ask students what role the players play in Risk, Fishin' Time, and Battleship. Ask them to name some other role-playing games. Other types of games involve strategy and knowledge but do not involve role-playing: Scrabble, checkers, Mastermind. Ask students to name some others (Pictionary, Password, Trivial Pursuit, Scategories).

Show and discuss the key elements of familiar strategy games (Risk, Battleship, Chess), communication games (Password), suspense games (Clue), and games of chance (Yahtzee), using the following questions:

• To what degree does chance/strategy influence the outcome of these games (25/75, 50/50, 75/25, 100/0)?

• Do these games end with a winner? What criteria determine the winner?

• Are the rules simple, involved, overly complex? Which types of rules are best, or does it depend on the game and the players?

• How much time is required to complete the game?

• Does the game involve competition, cooperation, compromise, empathy (intellectual or emotional identification with another)?

• Some games focus on a theme and players play a specific role. For example, in Clue the players become detectives. Other types such as Scrabble and checkers involve strategy and do not require the players to play roles. Name two games that require players to assume roles and summarize how they are played and how the winners are determined.

• Name two games that do not require players to assume roles and summarize how they are played and how the winners are determined.

• Think of a game you have played that involved cooperation as opposed to competition. Describe that game.

After your students have a clear understanding of different types of games, have them decide what type of game they are going to create. Discuss different games' rules, keeping rules as simple as possible. Then give the students the worksheet, which is an activity designed to help them practice creating games before they create their own game.

When the students have finished the worksheet in their groups, have them come together as a class and do the following:

1. List some of their ideas on the chalkboard.

2. Combine related ideas and erase the separate ideas.

3. Have the class narrow the list to the six they think should be included in the game.

4. Allow each group space on the chalkboard and four minutes to create a rough draft of a game-board design—the students should try to incorporate most of the six ideas.

5. Allow some or all of the groups to explain their rough-draft game-board designs.

Sample Worksheet

Exercise in Creating Games

Homework due by _____

• Decide on an end-user for your game (or use the end-user your teacher assigns to meet the goal of the lesson). Following is a list of possible end-users:

  • a local school's X graders
  • urban students in your state
  • rural students in your state
  • urban students in another state
  • rural students in another state
  • students in another country

• Design your game with the end-user in mind. Your game may have a theme that relates to your town, city, state, or country. Your group can share something about your lives with the student end-users.

Brainstorming (or Fluent Thinking)
And Other Types of Thinking

Once you have a workable definition of a problem or you have established a task and everyone in the group understands the basic facts, you can brainstorm ways to complete the task. Generate many ideas, allowing them to flow. Following are some basic guidelines for brainstorming:

  • Do not criticize any solution or idea.
  • Welcome and encourage "off-the-wall" ideas.
  • Your goal is to list as many ideas and solutions as you can.
  • Seek combinations and modifications ("hitchhiking" or "piggy-backing") of ideas and solutions.

Pretend you are designing a game about your school. With your group, brainstorm and list in the space provided below at least ten qualities about your school or school activities that your group thinks should be included in this game. Facilitator and checker, be sure to do your jobs.

Designing the Games

When your students have finished the worksheet and you have discussed it, they can begin thinking about the games they will create to send to the school you have chosen to link with.

Types of Thinking Skills

The students will use the following thinking skills to create their games:

Fluent thinking: Students generate a variety of ideas and consider many different approaches to deal with a specific situation or event.

Original thinking: Students generate relevant approaches but try to come up with unusual responses or clever ideas to deal with a specific situation or event.

Elaborative thinking: Students generate supplemental ideas to make basic ideas clearer. They develop a method of detailed steps to carry out a plan of action from start to completion. (It is part of the facilitator's job to guide the group toward this type of thinking.)

Imaginative thinking: Students visualize and build mental images of events or situations that have never happened. They try to reach beyond the boundaries of their present existence.

Group Assignment

• Brainstorm themes and titles for different games. Strive to come up with independent as well as related ideas. Choose two ideas and circle them.

• List some of the obstacles you may encounter in designing each of the two games your group has selected. List at least five for each.

Material, Procedure, and Duties

I will give each group graph paper, pencils, and a ruler. Each group will sketch a rough draft of your game board and any accessories (cards, tokens, money, spinners) needed to play the game. Your group should also begin to outline the game rules.

Facilitators: Take notes or keep a journal of meetings that are held both during and after class and be ready to report on (1) the progress of the game design and (2) group participation and acceptance of assigned tasks.

Checkers: Take notes or keep a journal on meetings that are held both during and after class and be ready to report on (1) group members' ability to express their opinions, (2) group cooperation, and (3) group conflicts and compromises.

Facilitators and checkers: Consider some of the following questions in your journal summary:

- What issues did you discuss?
- What positions did each member take?
- Who agreed to do what tasks?
- What things happened that helped move the group along?
- What things happened that bogged the group down or made it less productive?

Material handlers: Show your teacher the group's rough game designs and verify that you have all the materials needed.

Secretaries: Take notes and minutes on all meetings that are held both during and after class.

Group Feedback

After the cooperative groups have decided on the theme of their game and have completed designing a draft of their game board and accessories on graph paper, allot each group 5 to 15 minutes to describe their ideas to the rest of the class. The class can give constructive feedback related to improving the game idea or identifying problems using the following questions:

• Does the game adequately represent its theme?

• Has the group explored other ways of representing the game's theme?

• Does the theme of the game fit better into a cooperative or competitive format?

• Does the complexity of the game fit the age group for which the game is intended?

• Can players develop different strategies without significantly increasing the game's overall complexity?

• Does the game appear to be fun?

Finding Craft Materials

You can purchase the following kit from Create-a-Game, 1401 East River Road, Minneapolis, MN 55414. Materials to make seven separate board games cost $89.95 with seven game boxes and $69.95 without boxes. Add 8 percent of your total for shipping and handling.

You will divide all materials equally among the material handlers of the seven groups. Later, the groups can trade, depending on what they need for their games. For example, one group may trade fourteen missiles and a spinner for two dice and two large pawns. Kits contain

• Twenty-one sheets of graph paper and seven rulers

• One box of eight magic markers and one box of twelve colored pencils

• Seven blank 28-inch-by-19-inch game boards (14 inches by 19 inches when folded; regular game-board quality)

• One large bag of game pieces that includes

　　• 7 plastic bags
　　• 28 large pawns (four colors)
　　• 14 six-sided dice

- 7 spinners
- 77 poker chips (three colors)
- 77 missiles (four colors)
- 161 discs (four colors)

• Seven background adhesive game-board sheets (similar to material used to cover cupboard shelves)—six solid colors and one with colored squares (The creators can draw on the sheets with colored pencils and certain types of magic markers.)

• Ten 28-inch-by-19-inch sheets of construction paper—six separate colors

• Four small glue sticks

• Seven clear adhesive game-board sheets (to cover and protect the finished product)

• 210 card-stock cards (four separate fluorescent colors)

• Seven game boxes (optional, costs extra), 19.5 inches by 14.5 inches by 3 inches. These white boxes come flat so that the students can design them using paint, magic markers, or colored pencils. For example, a title over a game box design might read

MINNEAPOLIS BIKE TRAILS
Roller Bladers, Walkers, Skate Boarders, Joggers
BEWARE!
a descriptive cultural cooperative game
by Dawn, Sean, Teri, and Noel

If you prefer to find your own supplies for game materials here are some suggestions:

• Have students bring in items that could be used as game tokens (buttons, bottle caps, and so on).

• Buy construction paper, glue, token bags, and so on, at a discount or art supply store.

• Buy game-board material or a substitute at an art supply store.

• Purchase card-stock paper and have it cut at a copy center.

Crafting the Game Using Create-a-Game Materials

1. Each cooperative group chooses a color for the background and adheres it to the face of the game board. Fold the background sheet in half, then peel off the backing, line the folded crease up with the fold in the game board, and slowly and smoothly apply the backing to the face of the game board.
2. Each group draws their game design on the adhesive backing using colored pencils or permanent magic marker (be careful; the magic marker will smear until it dries) or cuts out their game-board design from construction paper, then glues the design onto the board. Of course, groups may wish to use a combination of gluing construction paper to the background sheet and drawing directly onto the background sheet.
3. When the groups have completed designing their game boards, they will cover the boards with clear, protective adhesive sheets. Follow the steps outlined in 1.
4. The groups custom design any game cards or other accessories.

Writing the Rules

To ensure the best rules for each game design, have the students write a rough draft of their proposed rules and then have them test the game over and over, looking for gaps in the rules as well as rules that can be deleted. Once the students are comfortable with the organization and content of their rules and you have reviewed the amended drafts, students should type or write their rules neatly.

Designing the Game Box

If you have purchased the optional game boxes, have the groups keep their boxes flat while they complete their box designs. Then have the students put the boxes together using the two-sided tape provided.

Have the students put the game boards in the game boxes and lay the bag of game tokens, game cards, and rules on top of the game board.

Cross-Cultural Collaborative Game Creation

An alternative to creating games for cross-cultural exchanges is to have the students from the linked schools create a game together. This approach, cross-cultural collaborative game creation, involves the same steps as outlined above, but the linked cooperative groups must find ways to communicate with one another.

The first step in this collaborative effort is to decide on the theme of the game. Then the groups will work independently to design the game board, but they will continually share ideas. They will collaborate in the same way to design the method of play. The groups will continue to share their best ideas with one another.

Through this collaborative effort, the groups develop a game and then test it independently of one another. The linked groups can share the reactions to the game and agree on what adjustments they need to make. Each linked group should work on separate parts of the game rules and then exchange them to let the other group edit.

Cross-Cultural Playground Games

A cooperative group may decide to create a playground game instead of a board game. They would decide on a theme and brainstorm in the way described earlier. Once they had completed the game and designed any necessary accessories, they would develop a demonstration to present to their link group. The cooperative group would produce an introduction and demonstration of their game using a video camera. After they had edited the video, they would send it and a written set of game rules to the link school.

As an option (or possibly in addition) to having the students create a new playground game, have them produce and edit a video of a game, activity, or sport that is popular and/or indigenous to their culture to facilitate cross-cultural exchange.

Resources

Boehm, Helen. "Toys and Games to Learn By." *Psychology Today* 23 (1989):62–64.

Botermans, Jack, Tony Burrett, Pieter van Delft, and Carla van Splunteren. *The World of Games.* New York: Facts On File, 1989.

Branwyn, Gareth. "Gaming: Simulation Future Realities." *The Futurist* 20 (1986):29–35.

Davis, Morton D. *Game Theory: A Nontechnical Introduction.* Rev. ed. New York: Basic Books, 1983.

Elder, Pamela, and Mary Ann Carr. *Worldways: Bringing the World into the Classroom.* Reading, Mass.: Addison-Wesley, 1987.

Greenblat, Cathy Stein. *Designing Games and Simulations: An Illustrated Handbook.* Newbury Park, Calif.: Sage Publications, 1988.

Johnson, David W., Roger T. Johnson, and Edythe Johnson Holubec. *Cooperation in the Classroom.* Goodlettsville, Tenn.: Interactive Books, 1988.

McNally, D. W. *Piaget, Education and Teaching.* New Educational Press, 1973.

Magney, John. "Game-based Teaching." *The Education Digest* 55 (1990):54–57.

Nesbitt, William A. *Simulation Games for the Social Studies Classroom.* Philadelphia: Foreign Policy Research Institute, 1971.

Piaget, Jean. *The Moral Judgment of the Child.* New York: The Free Press, 1936.

Ravow, Gerald. "The Cooperative Edge (Non-zero-sum Versions of Traditional Games)." *Psychology Today* 22 (1988):54–58.

6

EDUCATIONAL TECHNOLOGY

by Charles Fitzpatrick

A world community can exist only with world communication,
which means something more than extensive shortwave facilities
scattered about the globe. It means common understanding, a
common tradition, common ideas, and common ideals.

— Robert M. Hutchins

For a globally minded educator, precious few tools are better than the computer. The fundamental reason behind its importance is the same one behind the phrase every teacher trainee hears: "Tell me, and I forget; show me, and I remember; help me to do, and I understand." By taking part in activities through which they feel a personal stake in the lesson, students learn information, concepts, skills, and attitudes in a meaningful context. The computer is an extraordinarily powerful tool for engaging students and helping them relate to their expanding world in a geocentric way.

A vast and potentially bewildering array of computer hardware and software is available to teachers. Some of it is quite good; some is less so. None does much good when you simply plop it in front of a student. Just as textbooks have limited value if you present them in the fashion of "Here, this is good for you," so, too, the latest and greatest hardware and software lose the attention of young minds when you present them improperly. But good educational technology, if you give it a fighting chance to work and present it as interesting and challenging, can indeed achieve results not always possible through other means.

Simulations and Games

The hook of simulation and game packages is the computer's ability to allow students to manipulate information in their own ways. They don't even need to do hands-on work in order to develop a stake in the lesson. With a large monitor or an LCD projection panel and overhead projector, students can have the sense of being engaged at the computer even from a distance. For example, in the software package *Rice Farming*, by Longman, students simulate farming a small parcel of land through a number of years. Though the teacher does the keyboarding, students are engaged because they make their own decisions, tell the teacher what to type, then see the fruits or frustrations of their choices. Few urban American teenagers visit an American farm, much less experience the woes of farming rice with limited technology in a drought-prone region. Yet, through the computer simulation, they grasp with clarity the impact of drought, the effect of a well, the vagaries of marketplace economics, and some small piece of the pain and helplessness of scratching out a living in a situation where most of the cards are stacked against you.

... good educational technology, if you ... present it as interesting and challenging, can indeed achieve results not always possible through other means.

Through a great variety of computer simulations, students can experience firsthand the potentials and pressures, the joys and sorrows, of others' lives. The computer's capacity to store information can allow you to extend these games over several sittings, providing greater complexity, greater chance for long-term learning. Students can build a city, tackle immigration issues, grapple with revolutionary pressures, establish colonies, juggle the intricacies of geopolitics, tinker with global environmental factors, and so on. Each simulation can shed new light on current or potential situations around the planet, giving students insight into the lives and decisions of others, forcing students to face up to how they would deal with a problem, and giving them more cause to scrutinize the methods and madnesses of others living today.

Creators of simulations and games frequently build outside opportunities for substantial learning into the total packages. Many programs provide combinations of training packages and game activities that work in support of each other. Some very good software programs (such as *Balance of the Planet,* by Mindscape) provide ancillary printed material that is useful for extending the lesson, while others (such as Broderbund's enormously successful *Carmen Sandiego* game series) use the printed matter as integral pieces within the activity. Both strategies can be effective.

Another powerful motivator attached to these simulations is the potential to rely heavily on group work. Some software (notably the Tom Snyder programs, such as the *Decisions, Decisions* series) is designed with the constraints of a "low-tech" classroom in mind and focuses on engaging students in positive group activities as a part of the total package. The chance to do hard-core cooperative learning, face to face, while also engaged in a technological exercise helps ensure that students keep the technology in perspective—a tool, rather than an end in itself.

Data and Research

Group work can also be incorporated as a feature of another genre of computer-aided instruction—research. Working with packaged data base sets, students can explore a vast ocean of information about a wide range of topics. Integrated map/graph/data programs (such as PC Globe's *PCGlobe* or MECC's *World Geography*) allow students to investigate, format, and reformat great reams of data in many different ways. You may want to train students early on by assigning several students to one computer, so they grow more accustomed to sharing ideas and effective strategies. Later, you may provide more hands-on time for more students to give them the chance to explore the particular material that interests them.

Students can learn the concept of a computer data base and the power of its operation by creating their own set, using any of the standard dedicated or integrated programs (such as the data base module of Claris's *AppleWorks*). By deciding what pieces of information they need to collect, then seeking and entering the data, and finally manipulating the data, students learn the trials and tribulations of gathering data, the subtleties of decision making and research bias when entering data, and the power that can come from asking good questions of good data. The data-base environment is ideal for exercising higher-order thinking skills—application, analysis, synthesis, and evaluation. Searching for patterns within and between data sets and exploring and evaluating the quality of the data are important skills that students can practice easily in conjunction with hands-on computer engagements.

Mountains of interesting statistics exist in data bases. The data bases are available either in print or in digitized format. You can also create data bases easier than before because advances in scanning technology have improved the speed, accuracy, and ease with which printed information can be moved into data bases. For many students, though, finding their own data and keying it character by character into an existing data base template is the best way to engage personally with a topic.

Once you have chosen a data base, you can choose from other programs that enable students to present the data in their own way. For example, students can create data bases of AIDS cases in the United States, then dump the information into mapping software (such as Strategic Mapping's *Atlas Graphics* or *Atlas MapMaker*), and churn out many different ways of presenting the data. Here again is a strong opportunity to combine intensive student engagement with high-level thinking skills, research into a contemporary issue, and development of data-manipulation skills.

Telecommunication

One way to access data and integrate activities within a variety of disciplines at the same time is to hook up by modem with students from other cities, states, and nations. Telecommunication combines the incredible capacity of the computer with the ubiquity of the telephone. While on-line, students lose most of the advantages and disadvantages of personal appearance and instead focus far more on the exact content and style of communication.

There are numerous packaged curricula incorporating computers and telephones. Some (such as National Geographic's KIDS NET-WORK series) are science based but involve significant forays into geography, math, and language arts, as well. These programs are splendid for engaging students in a whole range of hands-on activities that provide a chance to explore others' worlds. The chance to map a dozen teams made up of students from the same grades but from different schools in different environments around the country (or even the world), explore the same topics at the same time with them, collect and share data and observations and anecdotes, and analyze the data compiled by hundreds of school teams—all are powerful hooks.

Improvements in telecommunication hardware, software, and services have enabled teachers . . . to share ideas, stories, and information with students and teachers from around the country.

Such packaged curricula are not the only opportunity, however. Improvements in telecommunication hardware, software, and services have enabled teachers of any grade level, with virtually any computer, to share ideas, stories, and information with students and teachers from around the country. Some services (such as Quantum's *America On-line)* provide a great amount of information for students and teachers to use—news, weather, bulletin boards, conferences, encyclopedias, software libraries, and so on—in formats addressable through AppleII, Macintosh, or IBM. Teachers using one type of hardware can send electronic mail that teachers using another type can read. Those teachers using similar platforms and software can also attach files they have developed and send them across the country for other teachers to use, meaning, for example, that students producing newsletters on local issues can exchange them electronically with anyone using the same software. The files do not even need to be in English—any language will work.

Multimedia

Included within the files that can be shared electronically are files that access multimedia sources such as compact disks, video disks, and sound files. Any users sharing similar resources can look at, say, wetlands projects created by students from the Louisiana bayous, tectonics projects created by southern Californians, and urban development projects created by Chicagoans.

The staggering capacity of compact disks and video disks enables students to take advantage of amounts of information that could scarcely be imagined only a decade ago. A single compact disk (roughly the size of a 45-rpm phonograph single) can store up to 600 megabytes (about 1 million words) of information, and a video disk (roughly the size of a 33-rpm phonograph LP) can store up to 54,000 slide-quality, random-access pictures per side. Mixing and matching computer hardware and software with these resources (perhaps then storing the result on a standard videotape) provides today's students with an untold capacity to personalize presentations on virtually any topic.

The capacity for educational technology to enhance and enrich our understanding of the world is limited only by our capacity to make use of what exists.

Today's students, raised on a steady diet of high-intensity audiovisual stimuli (a la music videos) and weaned on pocket calculators and highly interactive personal, hand-held electronic games, may not be as intensely interested in older versions of "cut and paste" collages. Exploring and continually recombining snippets from contemporary multimedia resources (such as ABC's video disk *The Holy Lands* or National Geographic's *GTV*), however, enable students to redefine pictures of past, present, and future in the ways the students see them. Multimedia hooks are powerful indeed for showing students the connections that exist across boundaries of time, space, and culture.

Conclusion

The capacity for educational technology to enhance and enrich our understanding of the world is limited only by our capacity to make use of what exists. Barely tapped educational gold mines are presently visible and even greater potential waits just around the corner. As globally minded educators, we must prepare ourselves for a future that has even more information available, more capabilities, and more enticements competing for the time, energy, and attention of our students. It should be a goal of globally minded educators to create in our students the disposition to seek continually more ideas and information about the world and its peoples. If we can engage our students fully in this task on a long-term basis, starting when they are very young, it will become part of the paradigm by which they operate. Technology can provide an effective vehicle that can both engage students and be engaged by them for gaining an ever better understanding of our world.

Postlude: One Classroom Scenario

As a demonstration of how some of this technology can be integrated into a year, here is a recap of activities I conducted with eighth graders. The following plan should be used not as a prescription or curriculum guide but as an example.

Our eighth-grade curriculum covers geography during the first three quarters. After an introduction to geography, we moved into physical geography. Here we combined hands-on work (including dough maps) with atlas research and the computer program *Geo World* by Tom Snyder Productions; we used AppleIIC+'s and Laser128's. In this program, students systematically search the world for specific minerals (appropriately positioned), choose where to mine, and see their results.

Meandering into meteorology, we used National Geographic's *Weather Machine* to look at the impact of landscape on weather and the impact of weather on people. On AppleIIGS's and AppleIIC+'s, students manipulated maps and data files to understand ideas such as zonal air flow, jet stream, and orographic precipitation. The impact of weather on some people's lives was brought home with the simulation *Rice Farming*, operated as a single computer exercise with an LCD panel projection system.

We used AppleIIGS's with the National Geographic curriculum package KIDS NETWORK: *Acid Rain* to bridge between physical and human geography. We teamed with junior high students in a dozen schools around the country and a school in Moscow to gather, share, and analyze real data and essays using telecommunication activities. Although the package is designed as an upper-elementary program, we adapted and expanded the activities for this grade level and teamed primarily with other junior high groups. Our science teachers shifted their timing in order to study acids and bases while we tackled the related geographic aspects of acid rain.

With better understanding of hardware and teamwork, we moved into a research project using MECC's *USA GeoGraph* and the AppleIIGS's. Students received criteria for locating a new airport and had to select a spot, presenting their rationale through a series of screens combining a map, a graph, a data list, and a data chart.

The outbreak of war in the Middle East caused us to take time out to explore current events with the *Prodigy* telecommunication service. We used an overhead display (and a handmade 100-foot phone cord strung out the window to the nearest phone) to explore news as it happened and conduct necessary research in an on-line encyclopedia.

Having some familiarity with data sets, we explored patterns of AIDS cases around the country using current health statistics in a data base. The original plan had been to use the IBM lab and the data base module of Microsoft *Works*, but the lab was not available, so we used AppleIIs again and the data base module of Claris's *AppleWorks*. In addition to teaching about health matters, the idea was to train students on hard-core data manipulation using a small set of data.

From a few columns of data on the fifty states, we moved to many columns of data on all the world's countries, investigating global population patterns. We again used *AppleWorks* as the vehicle for exploring patterns and relationships between population, health care, GNP, and so on, on regional bases. As before, we matched computer work with map creation in order to see various patterns more clearly.

After exploring these population issues, students had the chance to modify global patterns using *Malthus* (by Longman) on the AppleIIs. I demonstrated with overhead display, then the students grouped around computers to try it themselves. Only a few were able to avert ecological and demographic disaster through careful manipulation of birth and death rates, energy use, food production, and so on.

Finally, we concluded our geography study with an intensive analysis of the airline industry. Five classes of students each had their own airline and broke into six basic groups for research. As a reporting vehicle, the students used AppleIIGS's and Roger Wagner's *HyperStudio* (2.1) to prepare a "stack" of interactive screens. I prepared an umbrella stack through which all thirty student stacks could be accessed. We put the completed projects in the hall for the school community to explore and had a steady audience of students and teachers for a week. Following that display, I loaded the students' projects and the umbrella stack onto a national bulletin board so that teachers around the country could access the work.

The whole idea of this plan was to get students to work a lot with each other through the year, to get them to work a lot with ideas, data, and higher-level thinking, to use personal engagement to get them to identify with the topics that concern people in many regions of the country and world, and to increase their comfort with various machines and software capacities.

7

THE TELECOMMUNICATING CLASSROOM

by Todd Pierson

We shall never be able to remove suspicion and fear as potential causes of war until communication is permitted to flow, free and open, across international boundaries.

—Harry S. Truman

Imagine, if you will, a classroom where students are "connected" to all parts of the world. No, I don't mean your typical pen-pal communication, although that may be a part of this scenario. I mean students working together on research projects with other students across town, on the other side of the river, over the border, across the ocean. Your students may be collecting daily temperatures and comparing them with temperatures in other parts of the world in order to understand the effect of latitude and seasonal variations of sun angle on temperature. Or your students may be conducting interviews with senior citizens to gather information on the community to share and compare with a partnered school and community thousands of miles away. Maybe your students are surveying their classmates about the types of pets the classmates have in order to compare the data with a team of ten other classrooms (are different pets geographic-specific?).

Telecommunicating isn't for every teacher, although virtually any teacher who puts her or his mind to it and has the necessary equipment and resources can do it.

Perhaps your students are playing the role of the Israeli delegation in a simulation of the Arab-Israeli conflict as they respond to demands raised by the Palestinian delegation, played by a group of students in Seattle, Washington. Possibly your students are word processing messages to their partners in Atlanta, Georgia, describing themselves and asking specific questions that they would like their counterparts to respond to and show in a video letter.

Students actively engaged in real investigations, applying learned skills in a way that makes a difference to them and to other people in the world—sound exciting? All of the above examples are actually taking place, and they represent just the beginnings of what is being, and can be, accomplished through computer telecommunication.

The Basics

Telecommunicating isn't for every teacher, although virtually any teacher who puts her or his mind to it and has the necessary equipment and resources can do it. I will assume that you have met the first requirement; that is, you have the basic desire to bring telecommunication into your classroom or school.

Telecommunication also requires certain computer equipment (hardware) and programs (software). Virtually any computer can be used for telecommunication, whether it be an AppleIIGS, an AppleIIe, a Macintosh, an IBM PC (or IBM clone), or a Texas Instrument 1000. However, you must have a telephone modem, which enables your computer to "communicate" via telephone lines with another computer in a remote location.[1]

1. Many modems are available and prices vary greatly depending on the speed of the modem, whether it is an external or internal modem, and the manufacturer. Plan on spending from $150 to $300.

The third requirement is that you have access to a "dedicated" phone line (a phone connection that is not multiline). Since the act of telecommunicating can, and often does, take place at times other than during your class period, it is not essential that the telephone line be in your classroom. In fact, in some respects it is advantageous for the phone connection to be somewhere else, such as in a media center, where another adult can help facilitate the telecommunication sessions.

You need only two software programs to get started in telecommunicating: a communications software program that runs your modem,[2] and a word-processing program, which will enable you to compose messages off-line and then upload them as files. (Don't worry if you don't understand the language yet; it will become clearer to you as we proceed.)

Although you don't need a communications service (network), it is really what brings classes together in a structured way and takes telecommunication beyond mere pen-pal exchanges. There are many communication networks available, and many of them have activities geared specifically to the educator. Chances are that as you become more versed in the language and ways of telecommunication, you will want to explore some of the diverse networks available.[3] I will focus on three networks that I think can bring the world into your classroom by connecting your students with other students in unique and innovative telecommunication projects.

Sampler of Telecommunication Projects

What do telecommunication networks offer us, the classroom teachers, and are they really worth the expense? (An average subscription costs $250, and the price often doesn't include the hourly rate for phone connections!) As you might suspect, I believe it is well worth the expense. Here's a sampling of some of what is available on three different networks today.

2. My communication software program came with my modem; others are free and part of the public domain.
3. The Educational Telecommunication Networks section lists and briefly describes some of these telecommunication networks.

IRIS

Do you remember the McGraw-Hill Information Exchange (MIX)? The MIX Telecommunications Network made a splash in Minnesota schools a few years ago, in part because the Minnesota Department of Education provided Minnesota schools with an 800 access number, and in part because the central computer was located in Eden Prairie, giving MIX the feel of a local project. MIX disappeared in 1989 when McGraw-Hill merged with another publisher, but it reappeared in 1990 under the name IRIS as a collaborative effort between an organization known as Metasystems Design Group and MECC. Although it had assumed a new name, IRIS continued many of the unique, interdisciplinary student activities that appeared on the MIX network.[4] Here's how the people at IRIS described the projects they offered for the 1990–91 school year:

Hot Stuff

Curricular area: Science, geography
Time lines: Fall, spring; 8 to 10 weeks each
Grade level: Middle school (grades 5 to 10)
Students from schools at different latitudes in various parts of the world compare the variations in temperature as the season changes. Classes report the local air temperature in the sun and shade, as well as the soil temperature in the sun and the shade. All participating schools graph and analyze the data, then follow with an on-line discussion of student hypotheses and conclusions.

Winter

Curricular area: Science, language arts
Time lines: Winter; 8 to 10 weeks
Grade level: Grades 1 to 10

4. In July 1990, IRIS incorporated as a nonprofit corporation and split from MECC and the Metasystems Design Group.

Students from schools at different latitudes in various parts of the world exchange written reports of their observations of the ways in which different local birds, insects, plants, and animals adapt to seasonal changes during winter. Students track the changes that take place from the beginning to the end of winter via a national map and submit creative writing samples on the human adaptation to these changes. Participants decide if they wish to desktop publish reports of their work.

Plant It!

Curricular area: Science
Time lines: Fall, winter, spring; 8 to 10 weeks each
Grade level: Suitable for applications in all grade levels
Young botanists grow beans, radishes, peas, and corn in a variety of environments and share the growth data with other classrooms for scientific analysis and classroom discussion. IRIS mails seeds and graphs to registered classrooms. A contest is part of the fun, with prizes and trophies awarded for the tallest plant or heaviest vegetable.

Waterworks

Curricular area: Science
Time lines: Spring; 8 to 10 weeks
Grade level: Middle school
Young scientists gather data on the temperature and acidity of local water sources and share the data with other classrooms for scientific analysis and discussion. Guest experts on acid rain will be available during specified times to answer students' and teachers' questions. An editorial team made up of participants will compile a desktop-published report for distribution to local news media and interested participants.

Community Problem Solving

Curricular area: Social studies, student leadership
Time lines: Winter, spring; 8 to 10 weeks each, possibly ongoing
Grade level: Appropriate for grades 4 to 12
Clustered classrooms around the country collaborate to understand and take action on solving a local community problem or need. Students learn goal setting, written and oral communications, creative thinking, teamwork, leadership, and other problem-solving skills. The students use these skills to address a selected problem concerning one of the following: animals, children in crisis, citizenship, environment, the handicapped, health and safety, hunger and homelessness, illiteracy, or senior citizens. As students create and implement their projects, a resource data base of ideas and identified local and national service agencies will be maintained on-line for the use of future participants in the conference.

Teleconnected Cultures

Curricular area: Social studies, language arts
Time lines: Fall, winter, spring; 8 to 10 weeks each
Grade level: Appropriate for grades 3 to 9
Geographically distant classes conduct research on their community, culture, sayings, folklore, and history and then exchange their findings in cultural packets. The program emphasizes cooperative work and collaborative writing. Packets typically include maps, videotapes, souvenirs, and handmade items. Teachers and students will decide if they wish to desktop publish reports of students' work.

Think Global, Write Local

Curricular area: Social studies, language arts
Time lines: Fall, winter, spring; 8 to 10 weeks each
Grade level: Appropriate for grades 4 to 12
Students study issues and current events of global concern from a

local perspective and then exchange cooperatively written reports and opinions with classrooms from around the country. Participants may choose to desktop publish reports selected from the students' work.

ICS (Interactive Communications and Simulations)

ICS originates in the University of Michigan's School of Education and uses the University's CONFER II telecommunication network. Offerings on ICS differ in many ways from the IRIS menu of activities, although the goals of integrating students into a global classroom via telecommunications remains the same. ICS simulations and projects are geared for students in grades 5 through 12, with an emphasis on the secondary classroom. Another very apparent difference is that ICS requires much more extensive student participation and, due to the interdependent nature of simulations, relies on daily time commitments over a three-month period. In fact, ICS literature recommends that simulations be treated as full class equivalents, requiring that one class period at least three days a week be reserved for background research and telecommunicating sessions. An entire classroom may function as a team within a simulation, sharing the time and energy commitment among all students and lessening the time commitment of any one student.

Following is a sampling of activities that were offered on the ICS network for the 1990–91 school year, as described in their promotional literature.

Arab-Israeli Conflict

Participants are organized into a number of five-person teams. Each member of the teams will assume a role of an actual president, king, queen, or minister involved in the Middle East conflict. Teams will write messages, press releases, and action forms that illustrate their interests as they come to understand them through the simulation.

Environmental Decisions Simulation

Students play the roles of forty prominent citizens of the world community, drawn from a broad variety of backgrounds and historical periods, whom the World Bank has invited to an international conference to examine the environmental impact of a huge dam that the government of Zaire proposes to build on the Congo River. Students also report to the conference on a local environmental problem and offer solutions, which become part of a data base of activities that will be provided to schools who participate later.

United States Constitution

Each student plays one of seventy public figures from the last 200 years of American history. The students are organized into five-person delegations and become part of committees that will decide to redraft or readopt articles of the Constitution based on the delegates' concerns.

Earth Odysseys

In early winter five travelers will embark from Paris on a cross-country journey through France and into Northern Africa. They will file reports on the computer network and the students will be able to request information from the travelers, ask the travelers questions, and engage them in uniquely individual explorations of the environments through which they are traveling.

National Geographic's KIDS NETWORK

National Geographic offers interdisciplinary packages that include student support materials, computer software, and a comprehensive teacher's guide and computer tutorial for the teacher new to telecommunications. In fact, the software that accompanies the package includes a communications program and a word processor very similar to AppleWorks. You can duplicate the software for students to use in a computer lab. National Geographic currently offers two programs that make good use of a network's ability to gather data from diverse geographic regions, enabling students to apply the problem-solving skills of a geographer in analyzing patterns and making discoveries. See National Geographic's *Ed-Tech* catalog for equipment requirements. With the exception of a modem, National Geographic provides everything else that you need in their package.

Hello!

Hello! provides fourth through sixth grade students with all the tools they need to compare their community to those of ten other schools that comprise their study team. Students examine the topic of pets (a universal interest for kids!) and the importance of geographic location to different patterns of pet ownership. Along the way, they discover their own global address, using an exciting computer program that enables them to move a mouse-driven marker to pinpoint their exact latitude and longitude in relation to political and natural features. Once students have collected the pet data from all participating schools, students manipulate the information by creating bar, line, and circle graphs and draw conclusions about the most popular, most unusual, and rural- or urban-specific pets.

Learning the global address of other team schools piques students' interest to inquire into other characteristics of the communities and schools with whom they are working. The *Hello!* program directs groups of students to develop a description of their community that they can enter into the program's word processor and post via the computer network to team schools. For one of the classes that I worked with last year, the word-processing activity was just the beginning of an effort by every student to compose a letter and send it to the school that captured their interest most.

Acid Rain

National Geographic's *Acid Rain* unit weds scientific research with telecommunication for a learning experience that enables students to see the dynamics of weather and acid rain precipitation. The package includes all the tools the class will need (including litmus paper for acidity testing) to measure the acidity of local rainfall, to post the results to an international network, and to compare measurements as weather systems move around our globe. As with *Hello!, Acid Rain* comes with computer software, teacher's guide, student activity sheets, and a student handbook that guides student exploration throughout the unit.

Costs

I've already mentioned that the cost of implementing telecommunications in a classroom will influence a teacher's considerations. There is another wrinkle, too. For many educational telecommunication networks you pay not only the cost of the network but also the cost involved in connecting to the network via the phone modem. Luckily, there are services available that enable you to call a local number (known as a node) that then connects you with a distant network computer for considerably less than if you were to call the long distance network yourself. One of these services, Sprintnet, costs $6.75 per hour. So what are the costs for each of the networks I've described so far? The following figures were for the 1990–91 school year. They do not include your initial investment in a modem, communications software, and dedicated phone line.

IRIS
P.O. Box 42588
Washington, DC
20015-0588

Cost: $198 (five or more on the same order, $178)
Connection costs through Sprintnet: 10 hours for $6.75 per hour

ICS
Interactive Communications and Simulations
Room 4116
School of Education
University of Michigan
Ann Arbor, MI
48109-1259
(313) 763-6716

Costs: $275 per 3-month simulation
No network costs are involved if your school can make a local call
to Sprintnet.
Scholarships are available for schools that can exhibit need.

National Geographic's KIDS NETWORK
Educational Services
Washington, DC 20036

Costs: $300 and up per package
Connection costs: $100 from anywhere in the United States

You may also want to try GTE Directories' *WorldClassroom*. For
information, call 1-800-950-4GTE.

There are several ways to use your time efficiently when you are
on-line (connected to the network) and the meter is running. One
time saver is to "capture" information and messages while on-line
and read them after you sign off the network. Most communication
software programs have this capability. You can also use a word-
processing program to compose messages in advance that you plan
to post to the network and then upload the messages (send them to a
network) once you sign onto the network. Uploading and download-
ing (receiving information from a network) are merely procedures to
transfer information quickly, saving communication costs.

Teacher Time

So you're hooked and want to get enrolled in a network, but you are still wary of the time that it will take, both in the classroom with students and during your few preparation periods. To begin with, all of the student projects run for a limited time, anywhere from 6 weeks to 3 months. KIDS NETWORK's *Hello!* and *Acid Rain* each last 6 weeks. But beware, once you are in the middle of a project, it will gobble up lots of your time in and out of the classroom, especially if you and your students are first-time users. It might be wise to identify a support person who will work with you on the project and help share some of the time demands. Be creative; that person may be your office clerk who really got into computers last summer or one of your student's parents who works for AT&T.

The goal of networks is to establish new lines of global communication for you and your students to share information, make new friends, and apply newly learned skills in a real-world situation.

A New World On-line

The goal of networks is to establish new lines of global communication for you and your students to share information, make new friends, and apply newly learned skills in a real-world situation. I look forward to hearing from those of you who read this chapter and become inspired to go on-line with your students. Post a message to me through any one of the three networks that I have described. I'll be there with students from Ramsey International Fine Arts Center and Washburn High School of the Minneapolis Public Schools. If you have questions and want to talk via that old-fashioned (and sometimes far superior!) form of communication, the telephone, give me a call. I'd love to share what I know and help you over any hurdles that may be hindering you from teleconnecting.

Perhaps the best way to close is with words that a child used to express her perspective of her world—words that reach out in an effort to find commonalities with children across town, on the other side of the river, over the border, and across the ocean!

> from Washington School in Faribault, Minnesota, to Parsons Elementary School in North Brunswick, New Jersey
>
> My name is Carissa. I am eight years old. My parent's are not living together, so I have two homes. My dad and stepmother live in the country. My mom and stepdad live in town. I have a sister namend skhannon, an a Dog named bear. I'm French, German, English, and Norwegian.
>
> My family clebrates many Holidays. too my family the 4th of July, Christmas, Thanksgiving and Birthdays are important. For the 4th of July we go to a special park and spend the day there. First we set out blankets and lawn chairs. The adults cook lunch and all the kids get to do whatever they want. When luch is ready we come back to the spot our family has wet up then we eat, and after that we stay at our spot and talk, Play games and do stuff like that until super is ready then we eat. most of the kids play more games until it's dark. Then we whatch fireworks after the fireworks we go home.

Resources

Billington, James H. "Library of Congress to Open Collection to Local Libraries in Electronic Access Plans." *American Libraries* (September 1991):706–9.

Clark, Chris, Barbara Kurshan, and Sharon Yoder. *Telecommunications in the Classroom.* Eugene, Oreg.: International Society for Technology in Education (ISTE), 1989.

Grunwald, Peter. "The New Generation of Information Systems." *Phi Delta Kappan* 72:113–14.

Mecklenburger, James A. "Learning in a Wired Nation: Bringing the School On-line." *Phi Delta Kappan* 72:105–8.

Potter, Rosemary Lee. *Using Telecommunications in Middle School Reading*. Bloomington, Ind.: Phi Delta Kappa Educational Foundation, 1992.

Roberts, Nancy, George Blakeslee, Maureen Brown, and Cecilia Lenk. *Integrating Telecommunications in Education*. Englewood Cliffs, N.J.: Prentice-Hall, 1990.

Roblyer, M. D. "The Florida-England Connection: Integrating Telecommunications in Content Area Instruction." *Florida Educational Computing Quarterly* 2:31–39.

Watson, Bruce. "The Wired Classroom: American Education Goes On-line." *Phi Delta Kappan* 72:109–12.

Weinstein, Shelly, and Susanne A. Roschwalb. "Is There a Role for Educators in Telecommunications Policy?" *Phi Delta Kappan* 72:115–17.

Wishnietsky, Dan H. *Using Electronic Main in an Educational Setting*. Bloomington, Ind.: Phi Delta Kappa Educational Foundation, 1991.

8

THE MAGIC OF CHILDREN'S ART

by Meg Little Warren

If Kambia came to visit me, he would be happy and excited. He would like going to the movies and watching television. I would teach him how to speak my language. He would teach me how to speak his language. He would show me how to do his chores. I would help him. I could learn how they grow crops.

—Jonathan, ten years old, Cranston, Rhode Island

Jonathan and Kambia live worlds apart. Jonathan lives in metropolitan Rhode Island. Kambia lives in a small village in northern Sierra Leone. Jonathan and Kambia will probably never meet, but the two boys have already become friends. Kambia's drawing of a game he plays, *Bo Train*, has provided the bond. *Bo Train* is the window through which Jonathan is learning about Kambia's life and culture. *Bo Train* is also a mirror that can reflect to Jonathan a new vision of his own way of life that is both similar to and different from Kambia's world. In this chapter, I explore the seeds of a cultural communication exchange project based on children's art and an instructional methodology designed for an intercultural classroom.

Bo Train   Kambia Conteh

Background

Bo Train is one of eighty-eight pieces of artwork, part of a traveling
exhibit and teaching unit entitled *See Me, Share My World: Understanding the Third World through Children's Art.*[1] The artwork and
accompanying instructional materials were recently piloted in
twenty-one Rhode Island schools, involving more than 100 third-
through sixth-grade classroom teachers and 2,100 students from
diverse ethnic, racial, and socioeconomic backgrounds. The school
sites ranged from one of the largest inner-city schools in the state,

1. This global education program was developed by Childreach, formerly
Foster Parents Plan, in cooperation with the Rhode Island Social Studies
Association, Rhode Island Art Teachers Association, Rhode Island College,
and the Museum of Art, Rhode Island School of Design. Matching grants
were provided by the U.S. Agency for International Development.
Childreach is an international sponsorship organization linking caring
people in the U.S. with needy children and their families in
nonindustrialized countries.

The *See Me, Share My World* teaching unit and art reproductions can be
purchased through Zephyr Press, 3316 North Chapel Avenue, Tucson,
Arizona 85732-3448. For further information about purchasing the teaching
unit or renting the exhibit, contact Meg Little Warren, Project Consultant, or
Jaya Sarkar, Global Education Coordinator, at Childreach, 155 Plan Way,
Warwick, Rhode Island 02886, or call 1-800-556-7918.

attended by Spanish-speaking students, to a small rural school surrounded by farmland.

As a manager of the pilot project, I have been fortunate to visit all the schools; sit in on classes where teachers were working with exhibit pieces such as *Bo Train;* review "response" artwork, writing, and research projects; see puppet shows; hear storytellers; taste international foods; learn games from overseas; . . . the list goes on. The creativity of participating teachers has been endless. The art from overseas has proved to be a powerful stimulus for learning about other countries and for the sharing of cultures within a classroom.

In this chapter, I provide an overview of what teachers and students have done in Rhode Island with the hopes that it might trigger art exchange lessons and projects throughout the United States. The most workable activities often come from collaborative types of thinking such as brainstorming, jumping off, and piggy-backing on other teachers' ideas.

Teaching Unit Goals

See Me, Share My World centers around a vibrant collection of children's drawings. The drawings have been combined with documentary photographs and charts to create a composite portrait of daily life as seen through the eyes of children in economically disadvantaged areas of Colombia, Honduras, India, Sierra Leone, Thailand, and Indonesia. The artwork, photographs, and charts serve as a catalyst and entry point to the multidisciplinary teaching unit. The goal is to introduce American third through sixth graders to their peers in nonindustrialized countries. The unit is designed to be flexible and to be adapted to different grade-level requirements while accommodating students of diverse abilities and interests. Upon completion of the unit students are expected to

• Recognize essential kinship with their peers in nonindustrialized countries by recognizing shared needs and interests

• Identify similarities and differences between their daily lives and those of children in nonindustrialized countries

• Give examples of their state's interdependent relations with people in nonindustrialized countries

• Discover how art conveys a unique personal sense of cultural values and social conditions

Organizing Framework

Under the umbrella topic of "daily life of a child," the exhibit and teaching unit address six universal themes: global kinship, food, education, health, work, and fun (games/festivals). Motivating questions—Where do you live? What do you eat? Who teaches you? What keeps you healthy? Why do you work? How do you have fun?—introduce each theme and provide a focus for viewing and discussing the artwork and photographs in a comparative framework.

Each theme (question) covers a set of specific objectives. For example, the first theme, "global kinship" (Where do you live?), involves locating the countries from which the artwork comes, distinguishing the basic differences between nonindustrialized and industrialized countries, discussing experiences common to children everywhere, and identifying local-global connections. "Food" (What do you eat?) explores the production and distribution of staple foods, including diets and causes of hunger in nonindustrialized countries. "Education" (Who teaches you?) addresses the issues of access to education, literacy, and learning outside the school classroom. "Health" (What keeps you healthy?) establishes connections between health and the environment. "Work" (Why do you work?) examines the role of children's work in rural and urban families in nonindustrialized countries. The concluding question (How do you have fun?) enables students to celebrate the universality and diversity of festivals and games.

"The magic is in the connection made between you and the artist across time and space."

Instructional Approaches

The children's artwork and the spontaneous expression of students' reactions to the drawings are the starting points for the lessons. As one teacher put it to her colleagues at a school in-service session, "Do not dwell on facts. This whole project is about feelings [that arise from viewing] original art and should be fun."

Open-ended questions—Which picture do you like best? What do you see? How does it make you feel?—have encouraged creative and original thinking. Following is one fifth-grader's response to the questions:

> Picture I [liked] the most: *Goodness* by Malida Kood-oua from Thailand. I saw that even though people are different, they are special in their own little way. I saw how other people around the world live differently. Some people might think that the way I live is different from the way they live. I felt useful because I could help other people understand something in Spanish.

Children see different things in the artwork depending on their own background and experience. There is no "correct" answer to the open-ended questions. The message of a piece unfolds through the bond that the viewer creates with the artist. According to the exhibit designer, Randy Harelson, "The magic is in the connection made between you and the artist across time and space."

Typically the artwork and photographs are placed in a central location, such as a school foyer, library, or cafeteria. On viewing the artwork for the first time, many students have been surprised and have been forced to reexamine their preconceptions of people in nonindustrialized countries, preconceptions that are based on television and other media images:

> I used to think it was all death and sorrow, but it isn't.
>
> Even though the kids are poor they have just as good talents.
>
> They are not as different from me as I thought.

127

Teachers have followed up in the classroom with sequenced lessons, using hands-on prints of the children's art and a variety of learning activities.

At Clayville School, fourth-, fifth-, and sixth-grade teachers and the librarian took an in-service day to plan an integrated unit based on *See Me, Share My World*. They started the process by creating a web chart.

According to the sixth-grade teacher at Meadowbrook Farms School, *See Me, Share My World* is more than just visuals. The program lends itself to great flexibility in incorporating content and higher-order thinking skills in all areas of the curriculum. Here is her list of multidisciplinary activities:

• Discuss children's drawings from different countries.

• Locate the countries from which the artwork comes and practice other basic map skills.

• Create artwork comparing own daily life with that of children from nonindustrialized countries.

• Write and perform a dramatic biography of what life is like for a child in a nonindustrialized country.

• Read folktales from various countries (students choose the one they like and develop it into a play or puppet show).

• Have a storyteller tell African folktales.

• Invite guest speakers from other countries and people who have visited nonindustrialized countries.

• Bring in everyday products to create a display of global connections.

• Analyze import/export links and other economic ties.

• Make pie and bar graphs using statistics.

• Play games from different countries.

• Make various crafts from different countries (students choose the one they want to make).

• Put together a cookbook containing recipes from various countries.

• Develop a Children's Bill of Rights.

• Have an International Festival with samples of all of these activities to conclude the program.

Response to Artwork and Writing

Students respond to the thematic questions by drawing and writing and then compare their experiences with those of peers in nonindustrialized countries. Following are several examples of how students responded to the different questions and how teachers used the *See Me, Share My World* unit in their classrooms.

In response to the question, "What do you eat?" Yovanny Sanclemente Restrepo from Colombia created the artwork *Farming* and wrote, "In my home town farming is the most important thing we do. Our parents are farmers. They grow vegetables and fruit in order to make a living." A third grader responded to *Farming:*

> This picture reminds me of my aunt and uncle in Laos and Thailand. They always took me to the garden. My aunt told me if the corn is ripe, pick it. She told me she will take me to the store to sell it. When we got home we made soup. My aunt say I am a good helper. My aunt say that we will not have a birthday party here, 'cause I was coming to America. I told her that I do not want to go. She told me that I have to go, 'cause I will have a better life. You can eat ice cream, pizza, and other stuff.
>
> But are you going, too? She say no. I have to take care of the corn, mango, pear, peach and the stuff you like. When you come back you will eat it.
>
> One day she went to the garden and I did not go. My mom and dad said that we will leave tomorrow. We left and got here. My brother was crying. I say don't cry. I miss my country too. Our parents love our country no matter what happens to it.

The teacher of this student explained that the student's response to the exhibit art was typical of many of the recent immigrants in the class. Normally, these students were quiet and did not share their backgrounds freely. However, there was something special about the art. "It drew stories out of them. They had something inside and wanted to be heard." It was also important for the other students to hear the stories of their classmates who had recently come from Southeast Asia and Latin America.

Once students identify or personally engage with the images in the artwork, they understand and will not forget the difficulties poor families face in order to produce food in nonindustrialized countries. One fourth grader responded, "I did not like that they don't get lots of food because they need it just as much as we do. They work so long and they only make a little bit of money to buy a tiny bit of food."

Satpal Singh, from New Delhi, India, responded to the question "Who teaches you?" by creating *Classroom Scene*. Of it, he wrote,

> This is the scene of a classroom. A teacher is teaching the class. Two boys are being penalized for not doing their work. A student is standing with his hands up and another has caught his ears from his hands below the legs [called "hen," which is a punishment given in India]. The rest of the students are sitting on the mats. The Hindi letters, in Devnagiri script, have been written on the blackboard.

A fourth grader responded:

> Free Time. It's the end of the day and everyone is having free time. Everyone is all done with their work. At 2:45 p.m. we get dismissed. It is now 2:30 p.m.

The teacher of this fourth-grade student focused on similarities and differences between her class and the one in Satpal by asking, "How is our classroom alike or different from the one in India?" Students first made two lists, one titled "Alike" and the other "Different," and then drew their pictures. They became aware of many of the details they have in their room, including books, educational equipment, and numerous other learning aids, in contrast to the lack of supplies in the classroom in Satpal. Punishment was, of course, a subject of great interest to all the students.

Kambia Conteh in Sierra Leone answered the question "How do you have fun?" by creating *Bo Train*. Of it, he wrote,

> We play this game during moon light. We join hands and move round and round singing: Alata-lata, alata-lata gbamulata, Alata-lata-lata gbamulata, Alatao. At the end

of the song everybody should remain still. Anyone who
moves loses the game. This is continued until only one
person remains as the winner.

A fourth grader wrote in response, "I was surprised that the kids are
like us and that they have fun, too." A fifth grader wrote, "I learned
that you could have fun without having money."

One teacher had her sixth-grade class learn how to play Bo Train.
They then thought of games they played that were similar, drew
pictures of the games, and wrote down the instructions. Here's how
you play "Going to Pawtucket":

> You have to get some friends. And then you have to
> get in a circle. Somebody has to get in the middle. Then
> you sing this song:

> I was going to Pawtucket.
> I was going to the fair
> To see a señorita
> With a flower in her hair.
> Oh shake it to the bottom,
> Shake it to the top,
> For all the boys around the block
> To see your underwear.

> While you sing this song, everyone claps their hands.
> The person in the center turns and shakes. When the song
> stops, the person points to someone. The people then
> change places.

Culminating Activities

The final question, "How do you have fun?" brings closure to the
unit. Some classes have produced an end-product: class books combining artwork and writing, a mural, or their own *See Me, Share My
World* exhibit. Other classes have put on plays and international
festivals. Although fund-raising is not part of the stated curriculum,
students at more than one-third of the pilot schools have committed
themselves to some kind of social action project. Third graders at
Norwood Avenue School ran a Goodie Store and sent the proceeds to
Sierra Leone for school supplies. Fourth graders at a Calcutta Middle

School sold cookbooks that they created from recipes shared at their International Food Festival. They raised more than two hundred dollars for agricultural development programs in India. Every month sixth graders at Providence Street School in West Warwick bring $1.50 to class. Half pays for a Third World lunch of chili, rice, or beans. The other half goes to fund the enrollment of Amidu Sesay, their sponsored child, in Childreach's development program in Sierra Leone. Fifth graders at Wheeler School saved up their allowances and offered to do extra work at home to sponsor a child with a group of friends.

Students from five pilot schools testified at the Rhode Island General Assembly in support of ratification of the United Nations Convention on the Rights of the Child. Each school had developed a "Kid's Bill of Rights." Students from one school had collected more than two hundred signatures, which they attached to their document of children's rights.

Extending the Idea

One inner-city school with a large Spanish-speaking population was experiencing intergroup tensions. According to one of the ESL teachers, problems were trickling down from the high school. Students were echoing racial slurs heard from their older brothers and sisters. There were incidents between kids in rooms 302 and 308. Students would be walking by in the hallway and someone would hit them out of the blue. One student noted, "If you want to look at it the way the kids see it: the Latinas in this school are seen as keeping to themselves. They have a kind of tag on them. It's skin color. They're not dark. They're not really light—right in between." Students in rooms 302 and 308 had participated in *See Me, Share My World*. The two teachers decided to conduct a joint class based on some of the same approaches presented in the unit, emphasizing similarities and differences, observation skills, writing, and artwork. Following is a description of how the teachers conducted the unit:

We're going to compare and contrast; find out how
we are the same and different. Choose someone who is
not in your room. Turn and face your buddy. Look him
or her directly in the eye. You don't have to say anything.
For the next three minutes—no sound, you'll be concen-
trating so hard. Write down all that is the same between
you.

Okay, now talk to your buddy. Find out how you are
different. [Give students time to talk to one another.] What
did you find out that was different? How many found out
that the person spoke another language or came from
another country?

Does that mean my country is better than yours? No.
Does it mean your country is better than mine? No. What
does it mean? It means . . . if you come from another
country, you are special. You have something to be very,
very proud of. You know why. I only speak one language.
My buddy, who is only nine years old, speaks two languages. Two languages. She's special. What else? Here are
some things that my buddy taught me. We're all special, no
matter where we come from. We can all learn from each
other.

Ask your buddy where he or she comes from. Put the
name of that country on your paper. Take one last look at
your buddy. When you get back to your home room, draw
a picture of your buddy.

Afterward, the students in both classes exchanged drawings and
started corresponding with each other. According to the ESL teacher,
there was a big change. "Right now the students who were having
those incidents are not doing it any more. They write to each other
every day. They talk and say things like 'after all we've been through
. . . getting to know you in *See Me, Share My World,* I realize you're a
nice person . . . I think we can be friends,' and so on."

As a result of its success, *See Me, Share My World* will be expanded
next year to include an exchange between two schools in a racially
imbalanced school district. A pilot exchange will also take place
between selected schools in Rhode Island and schools in Sierra Leone.

The Magic of Children's Art

What makes *See Me, Share My World* powerful and innovative is the use of children's art as a primary learning tool. Art is a dynamic medium through which to learn about another culture. Drawings offer personal images about people and their living environment. The visual medium stimulates new thinking about students' own lives while motivating them to learn more about the countries and conditions depicted in the artwork.

Art can also provide a bridge between children from different backgrounds and promote the sharing of cultures. It is universal, transcending the barriers of language, culture, or class. It is a uniquely personal experience that appeals to students of different ability levels and backgrounds. Art immediately attracts children, tapping into their natural aesthetic responsiveness, thereby touching both the heart and the mind. Engagement through the children's art leads to empathy, caring, and social commitment, both locally and globally.

> *Art is a dynamic medium through which to learn about another culture.*

References

Carrol, Joy, and Willard Kniep, eds. *The International Development Crisis and American Education: Challenges, Opportunities, and Instructional Strategies.* New York: American Forum for Global Education, 1987.

Castelle, Kay. *In the Child's Best Interest: A Primer on the U.N. Convention on the Rights of the Child.* Available from Childreach (155 Plan Way, Warwick, Rhode Island 02886) and Defense for Children International USA, 1988.

Clark, Leon E., ed. "Teaching About International Development." *Social Education,* April/May 1989.

Cole, Ann, Carolyn Haas, Elizabeth Heller, and Betty
Weinberger. *Children Are Children Are Children*. Boston: Little,
Brown & Co., 1978.

Fowler, Virginia. *Folk Art around the World*. Englewood Cliffs,
New Jersey: Prentice-Hall, 1981.

Grant, James P. *The State of the World's Children*. New York:
Oxford University Press, 1990.

Hawkinson, John, and Martha Faulhaber. *Music and Instruments
for Children to Make*. Chicago: Whitman, 1969.

Hurwitz, Al. "Art Education: A World View." *School Arts*, May
1989.

Kidron, Michael, and Ronald Segal. *The New State of the World
Atlas*. New York: Simon & Schuster, 1984.

Millen, Nina. *Children's Festivals from Many Lands*. New York:
Friendship Press, 1977.

———. *Children's Games from Many Lands*. New York: Friendship
Press, 1965.

Rowell, Elizabeth H., and Thomas B. Goodkind. "Motivating
Reading Growth through the Joys of Art." In *Teaching the
Pleasures of Reading*. Englewood Cliffs, New Jersey, Prentice-
Hall, 1988.

9

CULTURE DISCOVERY BOXES

by Hilary Stock

No culture can live, if it attempts to be exclusive.

—Mahatma Gandhi

I burned my first (and last) American flag teaching a ninth-grade "non-Western civilizations" class in the mid-1970s. We had been reading the *Ramayana,* and despite the fact that our classroom was filled with pictures and art all relating to the *Ramayana,* the importance of the story to South Asians was not registering in the minds of my students. My students believed that only other groups had "culture," only other groups had cultural myths and symbols, so my students did not feel that they could relate to the importance of a symbol from another culture.

So I burned an American flag in class. I cleared a large area in the center of the classroom, readied a fire extinguisher, made sure the wastepaper basket had sufficient water in it, and lit the corner of a large, nylon American flag. It burned quickly and was soon sputtering in the wastepaper basket. From my students' reaction, it was undoubtedly one of my more successful attempts at gaining their attention. The subsequent furor over this demonstration was, of

. . . how the people of the world bring meaning and identity into their lives is perhaps one of the most important (and most ignored) questions we should be asking while developing curricula and activities for the study of cultures.

course, exactly the point. If no one had blinked twice, the lesson would have been merely a demonstration of fire safety and not an exercise about the meaning of cultural symbols, artifacts that not only represent an idea and a cultural group but are imbued with the idea itself.

We have a tendency to merge idea, name, and object in symbols. The artifact does not just stand for the idea; the two are one and the same. When I burned the flag, I destroyed not only a piece of cloth but an idea, an identity, as well. To prick the voodoo doll with a pin is to do the same to the person. Osiris, in the Egyptian pantheon, is the Nile, and the Nile is Osiris. We seem unable to keep symbol and meaning apart; the flag not only represents but presents. And each presentation is culturally rooted.

Follow-up questions to the flag burning were obvious: How would an Indian class have reacted had I burned an American flag in front of them? How would they have reacted had I destroyed an effigy of Ram, the hero of the *Ramayana?*

I present none of this example to suggest that the destruction of cultural symbols is a viable teaching strategy. Rather I use this example to suggest that how the people of the world bring meaning and identity into their lives is perhaps one of the most important (and most ignored) questions we should be asking while developing curricula and activities for the study of cultures.

So far, most curricula dealing with this area of study focus on the notion of cultural universals, the common aspects of culture that are realized in a variety of ways from culture to culture, the concept of culture with a capital "C"; all cultures have Language, all cultures have Belief Systems, all cultures have Institutions, all cultures have Economic Systems, and so on. Cultural universals are extremely important and useful concepts that are necessary to objectify the "weird" and "exotic."

But culture, with a lower-case "c," has driven much of human history. Today, it appears that French Canadians are not impressed by the fact that all humans Communicate; they care about communicating in the French language. The fact that all cultures have Belief Systems will not bring a solution to the problems of the Israeli West Bank, and Economic System is an empty concept to the *pepenadores* (garbage pickers) of Mexico City's dumps. What, then, are the aspects of culture with a lower-case "c" that groups really care about? Do these aspects include a geographic location, a specific language, a religion, ethnicity, or socioeconomic class? Or particularistic combinations of all? In other words, what defines my "American-ness," Yukari's "Japanese-ness," Mohammad's "Palestinian-ness"? Or are such nationalistic groupings too broad?

The creation and cross-cultural exchange of a culture discovery box is an activity that focuses on these questions and concerns by exploring cultural symbols and their meanings. Students in one classroom or school compile a collection of artifacts that they have decided represents important aspects of their culture(s). They attach to each artifact an explanation of why the class has decided the artifact is important. They then send the collection to a class or school with a different culture or in a different nation or other geographic region. The students also speculate about and write down the kinds of artifacts and explanations they expect to receive from the exchange culture.

If all goes according to plan, the class receives a culture discovery box from students from the exchange culture. The class then examines the exchange culture's artifacts, explanations, and meanings, and compares their findings to their list of expected artifacts, explanations, and meanings. In the process of the activity, students explore the importance of cultural symbols, learn through experience the reality of ethnocentric assumption, and are challenged by the joys and difficulties of cross-cultural communication.

In Wisconsin, rural and urban classrooms in the state have exchanged boxes, and classrooms have participated in international exchanges as well. Future plans include using the activity to develop intergenerational exchanges between student and parent groups.

In retrospect, the *Ramayana* and my India unit in general would have become more meaningful to my ninth graders had I thought of setting up a culture discovery box exchange with a ninth-grade class in India. Not only would my students have gone through the process of defining for themselves those objects and symbols that add meaning to their lives, they would have received a collection of artifacts and ideas from India that Indian students (and not an American teacher) had deemed most important about India and the Indian students themselves.

Creating a Culture Discovery Box: Observations and Suggestions for Grades K–12

Goals

• To create a limited collection of artifacts that the class has determined is representative of their own culture(s) for exchange with colleagues of a different culture
• To understand that one aspect of culture is symbols that the people in the culture share and the meanings and values those symbols represent, transmitted across generations
• To understand that the United States is a multicultural society
• To be able to distinguish among personal, cultural, and national symbols and meanings
• To become more objective about one's own culture(s)

Prenegotiation Activities

To help the class effectively negotiate what artifacts will be included in a culture discovery box, you must familiarize students with cultural artifacts and their possible interpretations. One of the best ways to do so is to use a culture discovery box a teacher has created.

The teacher creates a culture discovery box of authentic artifacts from a culture, geographic region, and/or nation. The teacher then uses these artifacts in the classroom as a "hands-on" activity that motivates students to inquire further about the culture. For example, a small group of students is given two large, pink, plastic clips from a Japan discovery box and is asked to brainstorm how the items might be used. Next, when they are informed that the clips are used to attach futons (cotton mattresses) to clotheslines and balconies, the students are asked to determine why, how, where, when, and who uses futon clips. Because the futon, which is aired and then stored during the day, enables Japanese people to use rooms for multiple purposes, the activity motivates students to discuss the geography of Japan (in spite of the fact that most Japanese probably would not have chosen plastic futon clips to represent their culture).

Keep in mind that teacher-created discovery boxes reflect the biases and needs of their creators. This bias is neither good nor bad but is a reality that you can use to help students understand the importance of the artifact-selection process. After exploring the

Students . . . come to realize that cultural representations are important, that they have a larger meaning, and that the teacher is not infallible.

artifacts in the discovery box in various ways, invite a member of the culture or nation the box represents to comment on the artifact collection. Doing so will be very interesting for all involved. For instance, a Turk found some items in a Turkish discovery box inexplicable—obviously not part of her everyday experience. A Kenyan deplored the stereotypical nature of artifacts chosen for a Kenyan discovery box. Japanese educators commented that there was too little of traditional Japan in a Japanese discovery box. Students thus come to realize that cultural representations are important, that they have a larger meaning, and that the teacher is not infallible. After all, we might feel a bit uncomfortable with a United States discovery box containing a cowboy hat, a plastic-feathered Indian headdress, a Mickey Mouse logo, and a cookbook titled *101 Ways to Cook Hamburger.*

Sometimes it is difficult to find a native of the culture or nation to offer a different perspective of the artifacts in the culture discovery box, but it is by no means impossible. Many colleges and universities have international studies departments, often with an outreach component that includes a speakers bureau and lists of resource persons. Moreover, many of these institutions have departments that deal specifically with foreign students. Foreign-exchange programs are also good resources to consider. Some state education departments are adding international studies consultants to their staffs, and these people are often aware of resources that exist throughout the state. A less obvious source for finding willing foreign resources is through state departments of development. DODs keep records of foreign businesses in the state. Often the spouses of foreign business persons are the best resources because they are able to commit more time to the classroom than other groups are. If the resource person cannot visit the class or if the resource person is from a culture that considers open commentary or criticism to be the height of rudeness, then asking her or him to list fifteen or so artifacts she or he would select to introduce an American class to her or his culture is an appropriate and viable alternative. Your students would then compare the listed items with the artifacts in the box.

This activity also depends on your being able to compile a culture discovery box. Compiling such materials for a classroom, school, or district is easier than it appears. Educators travel, and with some planning and leadership, you can exploit their travels by recruiting cross-cultural travelers to look for and purchase, with school or district funds, artifacts for a culture discovery box. Materials and subsequent curriculum development usually cost less than $100.00. (Many items also can be found in "ethnic" neighborhoods in larger U.S. cities.) The collection can be rotated throughout the school or district, benefiting many classrooms. Model schools and districts in Wisconsin that are dedicated to global studies rotate such boxes with great success.

Typical items for a culture discovery box include

- Newspapers and advertisements
- Maps (world, nation, city, subway, bus/rail routes, etc.)
- School calendars
- Age-appropriate books, magazines
- "American" products, such as McDonald's menus in foreign languages, Coca-Cola cans, etc.
- Postcards/Stamps
- Money
- Videos of TV commercials
- Age-appropriate games
- School textbooks
- Industry brochures
- Artifacts of historical importance
- Artifacts of religious importance

Student Negotiations

Students' choice of artifacts to include in a culture discovery box, their way of choosing the artifacts, and the reasons for choosing the artifacts will vary widely, depending on grade level and the cultural composition of the class or school. Nevertheless, if you are aware and lead your students, important ideas and themes will emerge. These ideas include distinctions and relationships between and among notions of ideal and real culture; subculture and dominant culture; personal and group experience; the intergenerational transmission of ideas and values; and the nature of economic dependence, interdependence, and independence.

At the elementary level, students have difficulty understanding the differences between individual experience and group meaning. Many times, initial ideas about what to include in the culture box reflect personal importance: a photo of the student's family (or pet), a favorite toy, favorite foods, a piece of artwork a student has created, and so on. In subsequent negotiations, the teacher helps the students categorize and generalize these individual experiences. For example, if five students have the idea to put photos of their families in the box, the teacher gives the five students a group assignment to come to a consensus about one way to convey the idea of family. Similar groups are formed to work on other student-generated categories such as sports, religion, and school.

The final collection of a rural first-grade class in Wisconsin that had negotiated in this manner included a Valentine's day card (for families), the sports page of their local paper (for sports), a school lunch menu (for food), a picture of the "class rules" poster (for school), a "Toys R Us" catalog (for recreation), and so on. The whole class then brainstormed how each artifact should be explained to their exchange class.

Their upper classmates, third graders, decided to include in their collection a plastic troll, reasoning that it symbolized their culture. (The village chamber of commerce had recently christened the village "troll capital of the world" and many local merchants were promoting the gimmick.) The teacher took this opportunity to help the class understand differences among local, regional, and national symbols. Would the troll have any meaning to, say, third graders in Milwaukee? The class renamed its box for the village and not the state. The troll also had stamped on it "Made in China," which led to a very interesting discussion. To what extent is culture determined by technology and the products one manufacturer uses? To what extent is the village "Sino-ized" by using a product that is made in a foreign country as a symbol of itself? Where were the other artifacts in the box made? In a roundabout way, the class decided that the symbols and the artifacts in the box had a special meaning to them—and it really did not matter where they were made.[1]

The second step in a culture discovery box exchange is for students to anticipate the kinds of artifacts they will receive from the exchange culture. Many times, even if the exchange culture is within the state or geographic region, younger children have been exposed

1. I found this conclusion interesting; it refutes a common American idea that the rest of the world is becoming "Americanized" because American products are part of everyday life in many cultures.

to little or nothing about the exchange culture. Such blank slates make hypothesizing interesting. The teacher can opt to let student imagination take over, enlist parent and community members as resources, or choose a combination of options. What is important here is for all learners to be aware of the sources of their information about the exchange culture and, subsequently, the importance of sources of perceptions about the exchange culture.

The procedure for creating culture discovery boxes in middle and high schools is similar to the elementary procedure. Sorting through artifacts that have personal or group meaning and finding out where each artifact is made remain important. But you can also explore

> *Students will . . . become more critical and objective by imagining the exchange culture's reactions to their selections.*

historical or intergenerational themes at this level. How has the meaning of the symbol changed over time? Why has the symbol endured? Will all of the class's choices endure? Why or why not? For example, there are distinct differences in two cultural artifacts selected by a seventh-grade class: a Teenage Mutant Ninja Turtle comic and a copy of the U.S. Constitution. Presumably, the turtles are a fad and the Constitution will endure. Having discussions of this sort during the selection and negotiation process helps students prioritize the meanings and relative importance of symbols.

Students will also become more critical and objective by imagining the exchange culture's reactions to their selections. Disproportionate emphasis on music and sports, for example, can spark debates about what is truly significant and representative. The selection process can be used as a metaphor to connect students to larger events as well. Islamic "fanaticism" is easier for students to digest if the class is asked to recall their passions during their own attempts to define their collective identity.

From my experience and observation, elementary and middle school students rarely even consider including artifacts that are negative examples of their cultures in their collections. High school students, however, do negotiate over artifacts that portray them in a less-than-ideal light, so you can explore ideas about real and ideal culture at this level. Symbols of divorce, teenage pregnancy, drug and alcohol use, criticism of the government, and environmental issues become items that the group will discuss in the negotiation process. A debate in a tenth-grade classroom over alcohol abuse is a case in point. After a lengthy debate, the class decided it was important to include in their collection an artifact that could symbolize alcohol use. Next, the class debated over the artifact; one group believed that an empty beer can sent the correct message, and the other group wanted a more positive artifact, a SADD (Students Against Drunk Driving) contract. After the students agreed to include the SADD contract, the teacher used the experience to reinforce previous activities concerning critical examinations of textbook bias. The subtle differences the class had discovered in the artifact-selection process between the meaning of an empty beer can and a SADD contract became a key to understanding why textbook authors choose certain photographs and terminology to describe different cultures.

The second phase of the activity, anticipating the artifacts the class will receive from the exchange culture, is as important at the junior high and high school levels as at the elementary level. Students will become aware of their sources of information or misinformation about the exchange culture: media, school, family, imagination.

Further Suggestions

• Set a limit for the number of artifacts that will be part of the final collection. Obviously, the experience has more value if students must choose only five artifacts out of a list of fifty possibilities than if they can choose twenty-five. Most classes send collections that contain between ten and fifteen artifacts.

• Involve parents. Not only are parents often good resources for information but, if involved in the process from the beginning, they may be more receptive to appeals for money. While the costs of developing a culture discovery box are minimal—most artifacts are free or very inexpensive—there are postage costs involved in the exchange itself. If the school or district is unwilling to pay for postage, a contribution from parents of one or two dollars each will cover costs, or students might want to raise the money themselves.

• Use each artifact the students select as a motivator for subsequent history or social studies lessons. For example, the use of mind-altering chemicals (represented by the beer can or the SADD contract) can be traced historically and across cultures. What role did rum play in the development of the United States, the Caribbean Basin, and Great Britain? How are opium and tea connected to the histories of China, India, and Great Britain? What are the consequences of the cocaine trade today in the Western Hemisphere?

• You can also use the process to assess student comprehension of the concept of culture and cultures. Students' anticipation of the artifacts they will receive from the exchange culture can reveal the effectiveness of a unit about the exchange culture or can provide guideposts for developing future curriculum.

Receiving a Culture Discovery Box:
Observations and Comments for Grades K–12

Goals

• To provide motivation for further cultural inquiry
• To explore the nature of ethnocentric assumption—cultural, regional, and national viewpoints and stereotypes
• To understand that a single collection of artifacts (or textbook or filmstrip, etc.) cannot portray the experience of a culture, region, or nation fully
• To understand that context and method are significant factors in determining results

Receiving a Culture Discovery Box

Before you give students the box, you must usually have the accompanying descriptions of the artifacts translated into English. Because

We all interpret artifacts and their meanings using our own cultural norms.

the explanations are written by children, sentence structure and vocabulary are often within the translation capacities of high school and college students. Foreign language teachers often find the explanations better teaching tools than the standard textbook fare. The explanations are authentic, often idiomatic, and interesting. Cross-grade cooperation of this sort is as educationally valid and necessary as cross-cultural exchanges. If you cannot develop such connections, see the suggestions under "Finding an Exchange Classroom, School, or District."

Perhaps the most important aspect of receiving a culture discovery box lies in the class's excitement and anticipation; they have actually connected with another (perhaps mysterious and remote) culture! But the actual lessons are hands-on demonstrations of cultural bias, ethnocentric assumptions, and stereotyping. We all interpret artifacts and their meanings using our own cultural norms. Student comparisons of what they expected to find in the discovery box and what was actually sent illustrate this fact very successfully. Elementary school students, for instance, anticipated receiving a drum in a Kenyan discovery box because "Africans communicate by drums. They don't have telephones." In their Kenyan discovery box, they did find a photograph of an elaborate ceremonial drum. But it was, the Kenyans explained, an example of sophisticated art.

A simple and neutral activity that helps students of all ages understand how cultural frameworks determine outcomes is to draw a symbol that can be either a 13 or a capital B. (Draw the one and the three close enough together so that the symbol can be seen as a sloppy capital B.) Then divide the class into two groups. Give one group a paper that has a 12 and then the symbol written on it; give the other group a paper that has an A and then the symbol. Ask each group to determine the next appropriate symbol. The first group will decide 14, and the second group will decide C. Although the students are given the same symbol, why does each group interpret it differently? Previous information—a number or a letter or a frame of reference (culture)—determined how each group understood the symbol.

After you have completed this exercise, the class can brainstorm a list of some of the cultural assumptions that led them to believe that Africans communicate using drums. Similarly, why did a predominantly white, suburban class choose a picture of Martin Luther King, Jr., to convey the civil rights movement and receive from a predominantly black, urban class a copy of the *Autobiography of Malcolm X* to convey the same experience?

Other factors of culture can explain artifacts in the collection and you should consider them: socioeconomic class, geography, the nature of the school system, the political system, and so on. Differences among the collections can also be explained by taking into account the fact that the exchange teacher might have had different objectives and collected the artifacts for slightly different reasons. How would the class's cultural artifact collection have differed had the teacher given different directions? You will also find opportunities to consider the differences between a stereotype and a valid generalization. Some of the artifacts included in the exchange discovery boxes are very stereotypical. One Japanese-created box, for example, included tea ceremony artifacts, origami, and a doll in a kimono, but nothing of

> *You will . . . find opportunities to consider the differences between a stereotype and a valid generalization.*

industrial Japan's wealth and prosperity. The general message of the box, gleaned from the explanations, is that Japanese culture is very old and very beautiful. And so it is, but the picture of Japan the students received from the box changed little of their perspectives. They had anticipated paper cranes. The teacher had anticipated models of Mazdas.

An important part of the activity is for students to understand that others view us in stereotypical and incomplete terms as well. You will have to develop effective ways of communicating this phenomenon to exchange educators. Ideally, the class should receive a list of what the exchange culture expected to receive from the class. Such a list would give the students insights into the ways in which the exchange culture perceives them.

The uses of the exchange culture discovery box in the classroom, of course, go beyond lessons about cultural assumptions and stereotyping. You can use the artifacts in the same way artifacts in a teacher-developed culture box are used. You can also develop a unit around the artifacts that will have more immediacy and legitimacy to students than a chapter in a textbook. For example, an all-girls tenth-grade class in Varanaski, India, sent five artifacts to represent their culture. You can develop a detailed unit on India using only these artifacts.

Artifact: A recording of India's national anthem
Curriculum:

- Rabindranath Tagore (author of the anthem), his poetry, prose, and philosophy
- Geographic diversity (rivers, mountains, and plains mentioned in song)
- Indian music, mother of our seven-note scale

Artifact: A piece of khadi (Indian homespun cloth)
Curriculum:

- Economic impact of British colonialism and the industrial revolution on the manufacture of South Asian cotton
- Gandhian economic philosophy
- Indian independence movement
- Khadi as a national symbol

Artifact: Poster of the Hindu deity Ganesh (God of students)
Curriculum:

- Hinduism: philosophy and daily practice
- Educational systems in India
- Religious diversity in India

Artifact: Photo of "hottest" Hindi language movie star
Curriculum:

- India, the "Hollywood" of Asia
- Film stars and regional Indian politics (e.g., Tamilnadu)
- Politics of linguistic and ethnic diversity

Artifact: Video of number-one-rated TV program, "The *Ramayana*"
Curriculum:

- General functions of myths in cultures. What stories, heroines, and heros would the class identify as important to their lives?
- The *Ramayana* in Indian history, humanities, and the arts
- Contemporary relevance of the story

If the exchange is between schools, different grade levels can compare the artifacts in their discovery boxes. For instance, why would a Japanese elementary school send almost identical culture boxes to each grade level? Could it be perhaps not so much because of Japanese homogeneity but because of a principal's directives to convey an ideal of Japanese culture? You can also use the collection to develop questions about the exchange culture, questions that are both stimulated by the artifacts included and the artifacts that were not included in the collection. You can then develop individual or group research activities.

Finding an Exchange Classroom, School, or District

International exchanges are more difficult to create than those within a state, and a good deal of planning is necessary. Will the exchange box arrive in time to fit into the curriculum? Will the time lapse between the creation of the culture discovery box and the receipt of the exchange box be too long? When does the exchange educator want our box, and how does the timing affect the curriculum? You must arrange and agree upon such logistics. Finding a contact person in the culture or nation with whom you wish to exchange and who is fluent in the exchange language and culture helps this process a great deal. Formal partnership programs such as Save the Children and Peace Corps Partnership Schools have such contacts in place.[2] Although these two groups require significant financial commitments, both organizations and contact people have proved reliable for creating cross-cultural exchanges. Returned Peace Corps Volunteers, a separate, national organization with state chapters, is also a great contact. Many returned volunteers have enough experience in their respective areas to serve as effective contacts, even if they are not in the "field."

You can find another more authentic source for such contacts through teacher exchange programs.[3] Often an exchange teacher is willing to set up exchanges, even if he or she has not been located in an interested educator's area. Communicating with an exchange teacher well before she or he returns to a native country is critical. Make sure you make as many arrangements as possible before his or her departure.

Some classrooms and schools have also set up successful exchanges using sister-city and sister-state relationships. These relationships are, of necessity, created primarily by interested and knowledgeable citizens and then formalized by the appropriate government agency. One can go through either the citizen group or a government agency (mayor or governor) to create an exchange.

Colleges and universities can also function as contact organizations. Any professor who is linked to an international studies department has contacts and may be willing to serve as an intermediary. Professors of education with an interest in international or global studies, however, are often a more sympathetic and helpful source. These professors have relationships with colleagues in a different culture and/or nation, colleagues who are ideally placed to work with teachers and schools to create an exchange. Furthermore,

2. For information about the Peace Corps Partnership Program, write Peace Corps Partnership Program, 1990 K Street, NW, Washington, DC 20526 to order their pamphlet *Educating through the Peace Corps Partnership Program.*
3. State education departments are sources of information about teacher exchange programs.

because the creation and exchange of culture discovery boxes is such a versatile and effective learning strategy, these professors are often the most enthusiastic contact persons.

Conclusion

Having attempted to put together a set of artifacts to convey to others a sense of their own collective experiences, students become more aware of the difficulties and subjective nature of cultural study and interpretation. The realization that their counterparts in other areas of the nation or world perceive them in incomplete and stereotypical terms gives students added insight to the patterns of their own thoughts and worldviews. At the least, the exchange gives all learners pause to consider our own assumptions; at the most, the activity improves cross-cultural understanding.

10

HIROSHIMA AND THE
1000 CRANE CLUB

by Walter Enloe

*That is true culture which helps us to work for the social better-
ment of all.*

—Henry Ward Beech

The white crane is the sacred bird of Japan. Legend tells that it lives
for a thousand years and that anyone who folds a thousand paper
cranes will also live a long life. Most Japanese children also know the
life story of Sadako Sasaki and the Paper Crane Club, which helped
to make the paper crane a vibrant symbol of the hope for peace.

Sadako was two years old when the atomic bomb was dropped
on Hiroshima on August 6, 1945. She was not burned, but radiation
poisoning caused her to contract leukemia at the age of twelve. Hospitalized, she began folding paper cranes; she folded more than a
thousand paper cranes with the help of friends, hoping she would
get well. She died several months later.

Her seventh-grade classmates wanted to build a monument to
Sadako and the thousands of other children who had died or were

still dying from the bombing. Largely on their own, they organized a fund-raising campaign. They asked children in Japan and thirteen other countries to donate the equivalent of five cents each. More than three thousand Japanese schools and hundreds of foreign schools participated in fund-raising drives, and in 1958 they had raised enough to build a child-spirited structure in the middle of Peace Park, topped by Sadako's statue holding aloft a crane. People place millions of cranes at the base of the monument each year. Sadako's classmates also formed the Paper Crane Club, which continues today and involves students in keeping the area around the monument clean and bestowing necklaces of cranes on visitors.

"Kids don't start wars. But what can kids really do for peace?" . . . the students were beginning to find an answer.

Years later I held the position of principal of Hiroshima's International School. One August 6 morning, the foreign children at the school and I were stringing together cranes at the monument when Kim Blackford said, "Kids don't start wars. But what can kids really do for peace?" Sitting as we were, surrounded by paper cranes, the students were beginning to find an answer. And so was I. Perhaps, if I would actively support the telling of Sadako's story to children in the United States and around the world, I would resolve my personal anguish over the inability to help, to do something constructive for Hiroshima and the bomb victims. But help whom? Affectively, at least, we are all A-bomb victims. And what we uncover from the past is a reconstruction that somehow is embedded in the present of our meaning-making. The message of Hiroshima or of Sadako is not simply in the past; it is the past in the present as future.

Late that afternoon I took the strung cranes to the Children's Monument and laid them atop millions of other brightly colored paper lights of hope. The park was alive with tourists, lovers, friends, and little children who were feeding hundreds of little doves. A group of Native Americans in full headdress were drumming a day-long prayer vigil with the participation of Buddhist priests and a South African "witch doctor."

156

I walked past the Peace Museum, which sits twenty-five feet off the ground on huge columns, like a tomb perched toward the sky; underneath there was much activity. Small groups of two or three gathered. Elvis played from a stereo blaster as six Japanese "Fifties" rockers twisted away. A young Japanese man with cerebral palsy and severely twisted hands parked his wheelchair at the steps descending from the museum to collect signatures and contributions to rid the world of nuclear weapons. "Was he a bomb victim?" foreign tourists invariably wondered.

Two young men with burr haircuts rode skateboards, and another, wearing a red-white-and-blue cape, rode a unicycle. They were U.S. servicemen on leave from the marine airstation where I had attended school twenty years earlier. What is sacred, what is commemorative? For whom? Were they exporting America's

The message of Hiroshima or of Sadako is not simply in the past; it is the past in the present as future.

carefree abandon in the face of inevitable catastrophe? Were they just ignorant, senseless, ugly Americans desecrating the sanctification of Hiroshima? German soldiers skateboarding at Auschwitz? Japanese sailors playing frisbee at the Pearl Harbor Memorial? Twenty years later, no longer banned from Hiroshima, these nineteen-year-old ethnocentric U.S. teenage soldiers were, if not welcomed, at least tolerated performers under the world's memorial to nuclear holocaust, part of the deep ironies and contradictions of and within Hiroshima.

The 1000 Crane Club and a Thousand Points of Light

I started thinking: Maybe we could start a club. Why not contact kids around the world and tell them the stories of Sadako and the Paper Crane Club? We could ask them to send cranes to be placed at the base of the Children's Monument. Maybe it would be the start of an activity that would help keep Hiroshima's message and peace in the minds of children all the time, not only on special anniversaries. One

Eleanor Duckworth . . . described good teaching as empowering children to have wonderful ideas and supporting them to follow through and actualize those ideas.

of the most compelling concerns of my children was that world media paid undue attention to Hiroshima during the week of the fortieth anniversary of the bombing, but that the media failed to tell the story of the weeks after. Would there be any interest on the forty-first anniversary or would the fiftieth commemoration be the only newsworthy date?

A club would give us foreigners living in Japan a chance to take part in the global community, communicating with students from other countries, finding out what they were thinking and doing, all linked together by a common project. It seemed like a good idea because, like Sadako's original cranes and the response of her classmates, it sprang spontaneously from a sincere wish to do something about a situation that seems hopelessly beyond a child's influence. It was a manifestation of social concern, of creativity, and of the urge to reach out across barriers of space and culture to become part of a larger community. It held the promise of taking the children beyond themselves.

Eleanor Duckworth, Piaget's translator and a brilliant educator, wrote an essay in the sixties titled "The Having of Wonderful Ideas" in which she described good teaching as empowering children to have wonderful ideas and supporting them to follow through and actualize those ideas. That was our philosophy. At the beginning of the school year in September 1985, the Hiroshima International School community voted that the 1000 Crane Club would become an integral feature of each class and of the school as a whole. Teachers would provide class time for the project, be open to expansion and integration into other domains, and would facilitate, but not dictate, what would happen with the activities and direction of the project. As much as possible the club would be "living social studies"— through hands-on project extensions, cross-age work and teaching, discussion of moral and social dilemmas, role-playing, arts and crafts.

We decided as a community that each member would learn to fold a crane, at least as a Japanese craft. No one had to fold cranes "for peace" (interpreted as folding cranes to go into the 1000 Crane Club booklet). We decided as a staff that active discussion of war and peace and the nuclear debates would arise only from the concerns of students themselves. The horror of Hiroshima and the anxieties of a potential holocaust would not be initiated by teachers; we would fervently support any discussion and exploration initiated by the students. However, the concepts of conflict and conflict resolution would be active and prominent features of our program, as would the study of critical thinking, debate, advertising, and propaganda.

> *Peace was a way of life, an attitude toward self and others.*

Part of our reluctance for a nuclear-horror approach to peace studies was that it was an emotional and cognitive imposition. Hiroshima City's Peace Curriculum, which we were invited to adopt by the city's Teachers Association and which was required in all elementary schools, begins in first grade with a typical lesson of showing children drawings of the horrors of war, including bodies in flames, with the admonition, "War is terrible! War is wrong, isn't it?" While we agreed with the evil and inhumanity of war, we were bothered by the admonish-and-scare-them-to-believe-in-peace tactics.

On the other hand, we weren't living survivors of the atomic firebomb as were the writers of the curriculum. From our limited (and perhaps naive) perspective, peace was not the simple abolition of war and conflict. Peace was a way of life, an attitude toward self and others. How can we help children to resolve conflicts more reasonably and humanely? If conflicts and problems are essential for growth, then collaborative conflict resolution and problem solving would become essential activities of our "peace club." Our greatest concern was to avoid talking about peace but to actualize it within the cooperative and collaborative ethos of our community. Preach little. Practice what we value a lot.

The students agreed that the senior-level classes would learn to fold three kinds of cranes, and these students in turn would teach the intermediate-level students, who would instruct the primary-level students. Peer pressure perhaps, but not teacher insistence, ensured that all students and staff participated. Students at the senior level also spent more than a month researching and planning their 1000 Crane Club booklet, which contains letters to students and teachers, the story of Sadako and the Paper Crane Club, and a bibliography of all materials on Hiroshima written in English. The younger classes made booklets and drawings, created murals for the club, and set up display areas for anticipated letters and cranes. Throughout the school, class discussions of actual and simulated sociomoral dilemmas, cooperative games, collaborative school chores, and the daily folding of cranes for each booklet defined the ethos of the school.

Sadako's story is the tale of the power of children working together in partnership for a common cause.

To publish the booklet and to pay for initial mailings, the students organized bake sales and a walk-a-thon. At a weekly school meeting they voted to divide their substantial funds ($6,000 a year) three ways: 33 percent to the 1000 Crane Club; 33 percent to school-wide projects (e.g., camping); and 34 percent to UNICEF. (Five years later, their commitment to giving to others continues.) On October 25, the thirtieth anniversary of Sadako's death, the club was born. Hundreds of booklets were sent to important leaders and organizations and to Sadako's parents and members of the Paper Crane Club who were present. Then we waited.

The story of Sadako and the Paper Crane Club is powerful on many levels. It illustrates a grim truth about nuclear weapons and symbolizes a fear of nuclear war that has been a part of many children's and adults' consciousness for more than two generations. It is also the story of a young person's patience, courage, hope, and creative activism in the face of the ultimate fear of pain and death. Sadako's story is the tale of the power of children working together in partnership for a common cause. Groups of students folded cranes, created a movement, raised funds, built a monument, and established paper cranes as a globally recognized symbol of hope and the wish for peace. The story thereby opened a channel for the creative, peaceful expression of fear about nuclear war in particular, and more generally, it provided a channel to express deep-felt concern about peoples' inhumanity toward others, as well as the hope for a better world.

Sadako's classmates started a project that has lasted thirty-five years and has become a tradition. It is a tradition that has grown primarily for the lived experience of its message. By that I mean that it is a cooperative and collaborative action; it is a nonthreatening, apolitical, humane way for children to express feelings that are ex-

Conflict, differing opinions, and even animated arguments are natural phenomena of authentic projects as students actively imagine, organize, plan, research, and implement a collaborative enterprise.

tremely difficult to articulate and resolve. And by doing so children can subtly, yet recognizably, let the adults around them know how much they care for each other and their survival. Finally, the work of Sadako's classmates, like that of the International School children's 1000 Crane Club, has served to give other children around the world a concrete example of peaceful cooperation and the experience of a collaborative project.

Conflict, differing opinions, and even animated arguments are natural phenomena of authentic projects as students actively imagine, organize, plan, research, and implement a collaborative enterprise. Interest naturally ebbs and flows among participants. Ensuring there is a balance between focusing on the "others" the project was created for and on the potential benefits of mutual respect and camaraderie from communal team work is often difficult. But the benefits are truly amazing.

The aims of helping and joining others in a 1000 Crane project, locally or globally, leads easily and naturally to exploring the relationship between international conflict and peace, between conflict and peacefulness with friends and family, between our personal "internal" conflicts and peace of mind. The project provides a natural context for the exploration of human justice and human rights and the environmental and people problems of the world. It provides an ethos for exploring the commonalities and wonderful diversity of being human, in all its interrelated, cross-cultural, intercultural, and multicultural forms. Working together and discussing, role-playing, or getting involved in conflict in order to find reasonable, peaceful resolutions create an emotional paradox that provides an ideal context for significant insights and social bonding in the classroom.

Whether children are six or twelve, folding cranes over an extended period of time provides a wonderful context for discussions and activities of peaceful collaboration. Whether for five or ten minutes a day or several afternoon periods a week, to think of Sadako or participation in the 1000 Crane Club, or to reason about a classroom issue, is to feel and reason at some point through various mediums about friendship, fairness and justice, prejudice and equality, empathy and reciprocity—in short, a whole range of hu-man values. Crane-folding sessions become a time to work together creatively, to help or teach others, to work for a common cause. And it is concrete mathematics (seriation and geometry), fine motor coordination (teaching patience, exactness and precision), and a won-derful craft of Asia (leading to other origami projects and paper-folding projects that originate in China).

Creative Extensions and Interconnections

Over the past seven years, thousands of booklets have been sent to schools and organizations in more than thirty countries. From sixteen countries, hundreds of schools and classrooms have sent a thousand cranes to be placed at monuments in Peace Park.

What is absolutely fascinating are the many wonderful spin-offs of this project, particularly the creative extensions it fosters in children and their teachers, and the interconnections made between groups of people. Besides sending colorful banners to accompany their cranes, groups have sent to Hiroshima hundreds of drawings, dioramas, collages, an original play, several video letters, tapes of songs (including original works), poetry, and stories—all expressions of the human spirit to create, to reach out, and to touch others. Numerous classrooms and schools and groups have linked with each other—in some cases classrooms within a building; in others, across town, a region, or a nation, and between nations. Locally and globally—interculturally linked!

In Argentina various schools throughout the country sent cranes and then began exchanging students and projects with each other. In West Germany a participating school created a cultural information exchange (video tapes, artwork) with a 1000 Crane Club school in Sweden. In Sweden a children's agency published articles on the club in more than fifty magazines and newspapers. In St. Paul, Minnesota, with a helping hand from Ken Simon, a class of second graders introduced Sadako's story to classes of eleventh graders and taught them to fold cranes. In a number of countries, including Argentina, Brazil, Mexico, and India, groups have translated parts of the 1000 Crane Club booklet into native languages and shared the story with other students. And in the town of Townsville, Australia, and perhaps in other locales of the globe, the whole town got together, led by the mayor, to have a picnic and fold paper cranes to send to Hiroshima. Inspired by Sadako's story, third graders at Arroyo del Oso Elementary School in Albuquerque, New Mexico, decided to raise money to erect a "sister" children's peace statue in Los Alamos, New Mexico, the test site for the bomb. Children and teenagers in New Mexico have formed the Kids' Committee to oversee the project. The Kids' Committee had collected $8957.93 as of November 16, 1992.[1]

In 1986, once the 1000 Crane project became a part of the school's activities (with the endless correspondence and delivery of cranes to Peace Park), I wanted my students to interconnect in new ways with other children. Over the next two years we exchanged culture boxes

1. Questions about the project, including how to get involved, should include a self-addressed, stamped envelope and be sent to Kids' Committee for the Children's Peace Statue, P.O. Box 12888, Albuquerque, NM 87195-2888, or American Institute of Architects, Albuquerque Chapter, 111 Carlisle Blvd. SE, #5, Albuquerque, NM 87108, ATTN: Children's Peace Statue.

> *By working together in a communal atmosphere of cooperation for a common good and for the joy inherent in the task of creating, children . . . showed adults how much they care to work together.*

and arts and crafts with a small school in Pigeon Forge, Tennessee. We exchanged video letters with other international schools in Japan, including travelogues and videos on indigenous folk dances and songs. We exchanged a how-to video with a school in Australia—we demonstrated Eskee Tennis and Radio exercises; they sent us a tape on Aussie rules football and the correct way to throw a boomerang and enclosed three boomerangs. And from a school in East Germany we received fifty drawings of children and scenes of "Peace," each under half a rainbow. We completed the artwork by drawing scenes under the other half of the rainbows, xeroxed them, and sent the originals back to East Germany where the two halves were displayed. And we continued to make tourist guidebooks (for children) to Hiroshima.

Over the years the Hiroshima International School students have raised the funds to translate the Sadako story into Japanese, Spanish, and Russian. In 1987 Premier Gorbachev sent them a telegram of encouragement. Of the many teachers who have written to Hiroshima International School, what is most striking is a common thread—this project encourages children (and adults) to enact social values not often given preference in our competitive, individualistic schooling. By working together in a communal atmosphere of cooperation for a common good and for the joy inherent in the task of creating, children, tacitly at least, showed adults how much they care to work together. It is a lesson for us all. Let me quote the closing paragraph of the 1000 Crane Club booklet written by Kim and the original group of children (now adults):

> Something we have learned from folding 1000 cranes is that even with a group of twenty-five students, it takes time to fold a 1000. In a class of 25, each student would first have to learn to fold a crane and then fold forty. But

once you begin it can be fun. Most important, it is a time
to work together, to talk about things like friendship and
conflicts. We don't have any particular suggestions other
than when we did this, we learned a lot about each other,
we helped each other, and now our class is really close.
We folded these cranes for peace and in memory of
Sadako, but really we helped ourselves. Please join us.

For more specific informatin on joining the 1000 Crane Club project,
send a self-addressed, stamped envelope to Dr. Walter Enloe, Institute of International Studies, 278 Social Science Building, University
of Minnesota, Minneapolis, MN 55455.

From Piaget I hold two recurring images. One is that everything
is interconnected and systemic. I look at a photograph of the Earth
taken from outer space, and I see a new paradigm for what it means
to be human. I'll tell you its secret. It's not the information-processing
system the scientistic education establishment wants us to believe
in—new machinery in an outdated like-a-machine paradigm. No, our
photograph is of an *umwelt* or ecosystem; not simply images of a food
web or water-oxygen cycle. Our paradigm includes two children, a
boy and girl, one from the United States and one from Japan, sitting
on the beach on a sunny day, alive and connected, and folding
cranes!

Piaget's second image of being human speaks for all of us committed to children as active creators, experimenters, and citizens,
locally and globally. We share with him the deep respect he had for
children and his conviction:

> The principal goal of education is to create people who
> are capable of doing new things, not simply repeating
> what other generations have done—people who are
> creators, inventors, and discoverers. The second goal of
> education is to form minds that are critical, can verify,
> and do not accept everything they are offered. The greater
> danger today is from slogans, collective opinions, ready-
> made trends of thought. We have to be able to resist
> individually, to criticize, to distinguish between what is
> proven and what is not. So we need pupils who are
> active, who learn early to find out for themselves, partly

by their own spontaneous activity and partly through the
materials we set up for them; who learn early to tell what
is verifiable and what is simply the first idea to come to
them.

In closing, I would like to ask you to join me in Hiroshima's
Peace Park. Imagine! We stand facing the Children's Monument,
dedicated to all of those thousands of children, who, like Sadako,
died from the effects of the A-bomb. We step forward to the monument and place our cranes at its base and read the inscription:

THIS IS OUR CRY
THIS IS OUR PRAYER
TO BUILD PEACE IN THE WORLD.

Resources

Levenson, George. *Sadako and the Thousand Paper Cranes.* Santa
    Cruz, Calif.: The Sadako Film Project, 1990. Video. 30 min.

Proceeds from the following products go toward the production and
distribution of the Levenson video. You can order them by writing
Informed Democracy, The Sadako Project, P.O. Box 67, Santa Cruz,
Ca 95063; by calling 1-800-827-0949 or 408-426-3921; or by FAX order
408-426-2312.

Asawa, Ruth. *Sadako and the Thousand Paper Cranes.* Poster. $19.95
    plus $3.00 for shipping
Coerr, Eleanor. *Sadako and the Thousand Paper Cranes.* $2.95 plus
    $1.00 for shipping; $2.25 each for orders of 20 or more.
Pack of 50 crane buttons. $8.95 plus $1.50 for shipping
Pack of 12 Sadako greeting cards. $14.95 plus $1.50 for shipping
Nasu, Masamoto. *Children of the Paper Crane.* Sharpe, 1991. $19.95
    plus $3.00 for shipping
1000 sheets of origami paper. $5.95 plus $2.00 for shipping

Skylight Video Productions. *Origami Video.* Video. Includes
teacher's guide and paper. Call 612 959-3544 or write Skylight Video Productions, 4456 Fifth Ave. S., Minneapolis,
NM 55409 to order. Videos are $49.95 plus shipping and
handling.

APPENDIX A

Organizations with Global Materials

Academy for Educational
Development, Inc.
680 Fifth Avenue
New York, NY 10019

Academy of World Studies
2820 Van Ness Ave.
San Francisco, CA 94909

Africa Fund
305 E. 46th St.
New York, NY 10017
212/838-5030

African-American Institute
School Services Division
833 United Nations Plaza
New York, NY 10017
212/949-5726

African Studies Center
10 Lenox St.
Brookline, MA 02146

African Studies Program
Indiana University
Woodburn Hall
Bloomington, IN 47401
812/337-6734

Afro Arts Cultural Centre
2191 Adam Clayton Powell Blvd.
New York, NY 10027

AFS International/Intercultural
Programs
313 E. 43rd St.
New York, NY 10017
212/661-4550

Alliance for Environmental Education
1619 Massachusetts Ave., NW
Washington, DC 20036
202/797-4530

American Anthropological Association
17103 New Hampshire Ave., NW
Washington, DC 20009

American Bar Association
Special Committee on Youth
Education for Citizenship
1155 E. 60th St.
Chicago, IL 60637

American Council for Teaching
of Foreign Languages, Inc.
2 Park Ave.
New York, NY 10016
212/689-8021

American Council on Education
International Education Project
1 Dupont Circle
Washington, DC 20036

American Friends Service Committee
150 Cherry St.
Philadelphia, PA 19102
215/241-7000

American Institute for Foreign Study
102 Greenwich Ave.
Greenwich, CT 06830

American Institute of Indian Studies
1130 E. 59th St.
Chicago, IL 60637

American Scandinavian Foundation
127 E. 73rd St.
New York, NY 10021

Americans for Middle East Understanding, Inc.
475 Riverside Dr., Rm. 771
New York, NY 10027
212/870-2053

Anti-Defamation League of B'nai B'rith
315 Lexington Ave.
New York, NY 10016
212/689-7400

Asia Foundation
2301 E. Street, NW, Suite 713
Washington, DC 20037
202/223-5268

Asian American Studies Center
UCLA, 3232 Campbell Hall
Los Angeles, CA 90024

Asia Society, Inc.
112 E. 64th St.
New York, NY 10021
212/751-4210

Association for Moral Education
221 E. 72nd St.
New York, NY 10021
212/734-6658

Association of Childhood Education
International
33615 Wisconsin Ave., NW
Washington, DC 20016

Association of Supervision and
Curriculum Development
1705 K Street NW, Ste. 1100
Washington, DC 20006

Bay Area China Education Project
Stanford University, Box 2373
Stanford, CA 94305

Business Council for International
Understanding
420 Lexington Ave.
New York, NY 10017

Canada Peace Research Institute
119 Thomas Street
Oakville, Ontario, Canada L6J 3A7
416/845-0479

Canada Studies Foundation
252 Bloor St. W
Toronto, Ontario, Canada M5S IV5
416/922-4149

Canadian Council for International
Cooperation
75 Sparks St.
Ottawa, Ontario, Canada K1P 5A5

Care, Inc.
660 1st Ave.
New York, NY 10016

Center for Conflict Resolution
731 State St.
Madison, WI 53703
608/255-0479

Center for Defense Information
122 Maryland Ave, NE
Washington, DC 20002
202/543-0400

Center for Information on America,
Inc.
Washington, CT 06793
203/868-2602

Center for Intercultural Studies in
Folklore and Enthnomusicology
University of Texas
Student Services Building 203
Austin, TX 78712
512/471-1288

Center for International Education
University of Massachusetts
School of Education Hills House
South
Amherst, MA 01002

Center for International Programs
and Comparative Studies
Cultural Education Center
Empire State Plaza
Albany, NY 12230
518/474-5801

Center for International Studies
University of Missouri
St. Louis, MO 63121

Center for Teaching about China
407 S. Dearborn, Ste. 685
Chicago, IL 60605

Center for Teaching International
  Relations
University of Denver
Denver, CO 80208
303/753-3106

Center for the Study of Development
  and Social Change
1430 Massachusetts Ave., Rm. 202
Cambridge, MA 01238

Center for World Education
College of Education and Social
  Studies
University of Vermont
Burlington, VT 05401
802/656-3356

Center of Concern
3700 13th St. NE
Washington, DC 20017

Children's Museum
Jamaicaway
Boston, MA 02130
513/434-7300

China Council of the Asia Society
133 E. 58th St.
New York, NY 10022

China Institute of America
125 E. 65th St.
New York, NY 10021

Citizen's Committee on Interdependence Education
1011 Arlington Blvd., Ste. W219
Arlington, VA 22209
703/524-4400

Concordia Language Villages
901 S. 8th St.
Moorhead, MN 56562
800/247-1044 (in MN)
800/222-4750 (outside)

Consortium for International Studies
  Education
University of Missouri
St. Louis, MO 63121

Constitutional Rights Foundation
6310 San Vicente Blvd., Ste. 402
Los Angeles, CA 90048
213/930-1510

Council for Intercultural Studies
  and Programs
Council for International Studies
  Program
Council on International and Public
  Affairs, Inc.
60 E. 42nd St.
New York, NY 10017
212/972-9877

Council on Anthropology and
  Education
1703 New Hampshire Ave.
Washington, DC 20009

Council on International Educational
  Exchange
777 United Nations Plaza
New York, NY 10017
212/661-0310

Council on Interracial Books
  for Children
1841 Broadway
New York, NY 10023
212/757-5339

Culture Learning Institute
The East-West Center
1777 East-West Rd.
Honolulu, HI 96822

Development Education Centre
121 A Avenue Rd.
Toronto, Ontario, Canada M5R 2G3
416/964-6560

East Asian Language and Area Center
University of Virginia
Randall Hall
Charlottesville, VA 22903
804/924-7146

Education Development Center
School and Society Programs
55 Chapel St.
Newton, MA 02160
617/969-7100

ERIC Clearinghouse for Social Studies/
 Social Science Education
855 Broadway
Boulder, CO 80302
303/492-8434

Experiment in International Living
Kipling Rd.
Brattleboro, VT 15301
802/257-7751

Foreign Policy Association
345 E. 46th St.
New York, NY 10017
212/557-8720

Foreign Policy Research Institute
3508 Market St., Ste. 350
Science Center
Philadelphia, PA 19104

Friendship Ambassadors Foundation
10 W. 66th St.
New York, NY 10023

Global Development Studies Institute
Millbrook School
Millbrook, NY 12545
914/677-5606

Global Education Associates
552 Park Ave.
East Orange, NJ 07017
201/675-1409

Global Education Outreach
159 College NE
Grand Rapids, MI 49503
616/456-3759

Global Learning, Inc.
40 S. Fullerton Ave.
Montclair, NJ 07042
201/783-7616

Global Perspectives in Education, Inc.
 (American Forum)
45 John St.
New York, NY 10003
212/475-0850

Global Studies Resource Center
6300 Walker St.
St. Louis Park, MN 55416
612/925-1128

Institute for Education in Peace
 and Justice
3700 West Pine
St. Louis, MO 63108

Institute for Environmental Education
8911 Euclid Ave.
Cleveland, OH 44106

Institute for International Policy
122 Maryland Ave. NE
Washington, DC 20002

Institute for the Future
2740 Sand Hill Rd.
Menlo Park, CA 94025
415/854-6322

Institute for Wholistic Education
Box 575
Amherst, MA 01002

Institute for World Order
1140 Avenue of the Americas
New York, NY 10036
212/575-0055

Institute of International Education
809 United Nations Plaza
New York, NY 10017
212/883-8224

Institute of International Studies
Outreach Programs
298 Social Science Bldg.
University of Minnesota
Minneapolis, MN 55455
612/624-6527

Institute of World Affairs
University of Wisconsin-Milwaukee
P.O. Box 413
Milwaukee, WI 53201
414/963-4251

Interculture Associates
Box 277
Thompson, CT 06277

International Association of Educators
for World Peace
P.O. Box 3282, Blue Springs Station
Huntsville, AL 35810
205/539-7205

International Christian Youth
Exchange
74 Trinity Place, Rm 610
New York, NY 10006

International Council for Educational
Development
680 Fifth Ave.
New York, NY 10019
212/582-3970

International Internship Programs
2124 Bancroft Place
Washington, DC 20008
202/232-0331

Japan-American Society of Washington
1308 18 St. NW, Ste. 704
Washington, DC 20036

Japanese American Curriculum
Project
P.O. Box 367
414 E. Third Ave.
San Mateo, CA 94401
415/343-9408

Japan Society
333 E. 47th St.
New York, NY 10017
212/832-1155

Latin American Studies Association
Center for Latin American Studies
1208 W. California
University of Illinois
Urbana, IL 61801

Middle East Institute
1761 N. Street NW
Washington, DC 20036

Middle East Studies Association
New York University
Nagop Kevorkian Center for Near
Eastern Studies
Washington Square
New York, NY 10003
212/598-2400

National Association for Humanities
Education
3534 South 108th St.
Omaha, NB 68144
402/393-0926

National Association of Elementary
School Principals
1801 North Moore St.
Arlington, VA 22209
703/528-6000

National Association of Secondary
School Principals
1904 Association Dr.
Reston, VA 22091
703/860-0200

National Catholic Educational
Association
1 Dupont Circle, Ste. 350
Washington, DC 20036
202/293-5954

National Commission on Resources
for Youth, Inc.
36 West 44th St.
New York, NY 10036
212/532-5005

National Council for the Social Studies
361 S. Wisconsin NW
Washington, DC 20016
202/966-7840

National Education Association
1201 16th Street NW
Washington, DC 20036
202/833-4105

National 4-H Council
7100 Connecticut Ave.
Washington, DC 20015
301/656-9000

National Youth Leadership Council
1910 West County Road B
St. Paul, MN 55113
612/631-3672

North Atlantic Treaty Organization
Information Services
1110 Brussels, Belgium

Operation Crossroads Africa, Inc.
150 Fifth Ave., Ste. 310
New York, NY 10011

Overseas Development Council
1717 Massachusetts Ave. NW, Ste. 501
Washington, DC 20036

Oxfam-America Inc.
302 Columbus Ave.
Boston, MA 02116
617/247-3304

Partners of Americas
20001 S. Street, NW
Washington, DC 20009
202/332-7332

Pennsylvania Council for International
Education
Beaver College
Glenside, PA 19038
215/884-3500

People-to-People International
Crown Center
2440 Pershing Rd.
Kansas City, MO 64108

Population Institute
110 Maryland Ave. NE
Washington, DC 20002
202/554-3300

Population Reference Bureau
1337 Connecticut Ave. NW
Washington, DC 20036
202/785-4664

Simile II
218 12th St./P.O. Box 910
Del Mar, CA 92014
714/755-0272

Sister Cities International
1625 Eye St., NW, Ste. 424-26
Washington, DC 20006
202/293-5504

Social Science Educational Consortium Inc.
855 Broadway
Boulder, CO 80302

Society for Intercultural Education,
Training and Research
Georgetown University
Washington, DC 20047

Society for Intercultural Education,
Training and Research
Intercultural Communications
Network
107 M1B University of Pittsburgh
Pittsburgh, PA 15260

Teaching Japan in the Schools
Rogers House
549 Salvatierra St.
Stanford, CA 94305

The United Nations Association
of the United States of America
485 5th Ave.
NY, NY 10017
212/697-3232

U.S. Committee for UNICEF
331 E. 38th St.
New York, NY 10016
212/686-5522

United States National Commission
for UNESCO
Department of State
Washington, DC 20520
202/632-2750

U.S. Office of Education
Division of International Education
Department of Health, Education and
    Welfare
Washington, DC 20202
202/245-9692

Washington International School
(lower school) 2735 Olive St. NW
Washington, DC 20007
202/333-8510
(upper school) 3100 Macomb St. NW
Washington DC 20008
202/966-8510

Women in World Area Studies
6300 Walker St.
St. Louis Park, MN 55426
612/925-4300

Women's International League for Peace
    and Freedom
1213 Race St.
Philadelphia, PA 19107
215/563-7110

World Bank Educational Publications
1818 H St., NW
Washington, DC 20433

World Council of Churches
Participation in Development
150 Route De Ferney
1211 Geneva 20, Switzerland

World Eagle
64 Washburn Ave.
Wellesley, MA 02181

World Education
1414 Avenue of the Americas
New York, NY 10019
212/838-5255

World Future Society
4916 St. Elmo Ave.
Washington, DC 20014

World Game
3500 Market St.
Philadelphia, PA 19104
215/387-5400

World Religions Curriculum
    Development Center
6300 Walker St. Rm 228
St. Louis Park, MN 55416
612/925-1776

Worldwatch Institute
1776 Massachusetts Ave. NW
Washington, DC 20036

World Without War Council, Inc.
67 East Madison
Chicago, IL 60603
312/236-7459

APPENDIX B
U.S. Addresses of Foreign Embassies

Afghanistan
2341 Wyoming Ave., NW, Washington, DC 20008

Algeria
2118 Kalorama Rd., Washington, DC 20008

Andorra
1923 W. Irving Park Rd., Chicago, IL 60613

Anguilla
c/o Tromson Monroe, Inc., 40 E. 49th St., New York, NY 10017

Antigua
610 Fifth Ave., Suite 311, New York, NY 10020

Argentina
1600 New Hampshire Ave., NW, Washington, DC 20009

Aruba
1270 Avenue of the Americas, Rm. 2212, New York, NY 10020

Australia
1601 Massachusetts Ave., NW, Washington, DC 20036

Austria
2343 Massachusetts Ave., NW, Washington, DC 20008

Bahamas
600 New Hampshire Ave., NW, Washington, DC 20037

Bahrain
3502 International Dr., NW, Washington, DC 20008

Bangladesh
2201 Wisconsin Ave., NW, Ste. 300, Washington, DC 20007

Barbados
2144 Wyoming Ave., NW, Washington, DC 20008

Barbuda
610 Fifth Ave., Ste. 311, New York, NY 10020

Belgium
3330 Gaarfield St. NW, Washington, DC 20008

Belize
1129 20th St. NW, Washington, DC 20036

Benin
2737 Cathedral Ave., NW, Washington, DC 20008

Bhutan
2 United Nations Plaza, 27th Fl., New York, NY 10017

Bolivia
3014 Massachusetts Ave., NW, Washington, DC 20008

Botswana
4301 Connecticut Ave., NW, Ste. 404, Washington, DC 20008

Brazil
3006 Massachusetts Ave., NW, Washington, DC 20008

Brunei Darussalam
Watergate, 2600 Virginia Ave., Ste. 300, Washington, DC 20037

Bulgaria
1621 22nd St. NW, Washington, DC 20008

Burkina Faso (formerly Upper Volta)
2340 Massachusetts Ave., NW, Washington, DC 20008

Burma
  2300 S. St. NW, Washington, DC
  20008

Burundi (Republic of)
  2233 Wisconsin Ave., NW, Washington, DC 20007

Cameroon Republic
  2349 Massachusetts Ave., NW,
  Washington, DC 20008

Canada
  1746 Massachusetts, Ave., NW,
  Washington, DC 20036

Cape Verde Islands
  3415 Massachusetts Ave., NW,
  Washington, DC 20007

Central African Republic
  1618 22nd St. NW, Washington, DC
  20008

Chad (Republic of)
  2002 R St. NW, Washington, DC
  20009

Chile
  1732 Massachusetts Ave., NW,
  Washington, DC 20036

China, People's Republic of
  2300 Connecticut Ave., NW,
  Washington, DC 20008

Colombia
  2118 Leroy Place, NW, Washington, DC 20008

Congo
  2891 Colorado Ave., NW, Washington, DC 20011

Costa Rica
  2112 S. St. NW, Washington, DC
  20008

Cuba
  315 Lexington Ave., New York, NY
  10016

Cyprus
  2211 R St. NW, Washington, DC
  20008

Cyprus (controlled by Turkish
  Community)
  821 United Nations Plaza, 6th Fl.,
  New York, NY 10017

Czechoslovakia
  3900 Linnean Ave., NW, Washington, DC 20008

Denmark (includes Greenland)
  3200 Whitehaven St. NW, Washington, DC 20008

Djibouti
  866 United Nations Plaza, New
  York, NY 10017

Dominica
  20 E. 46th St., New York, NY 10017

Dominican Republic
  1715 22nd St. NW, Washington, DC
  20008

Ecuador
  2535 15th St. NW, Washington, DC
  20009

Egypt
  2310 Decatur Pl. NW, Washington,
  DC 20008

El Salvador
  2308 California St. NW, Washington,
  DC 20008

Equatorial Guinea
  801 Second Ave., New York, NY
  10017

Estonia
  9 Rockefeller Plaza, New York, NY
  10020

Ethiopia
  2134 Kalorama Rd. NW, Washington, DC 20008

Fiji Islands
  1140 19th St., 6th Fl, Washington,
  DC 20036

Finland
  3216 New Mexico Ave. NW,
  Washington, DC 20016

France
4101 Reservoir Rd. NW, Washington
DC 20007

Gabon
20334 20th St. NW, Washington, DC
20009

Gambia
1785 Massachusetts Ave. NW,
Washington, DC 20036

German Democratic Republic (East
Germany)
1717 Massachusetts Ave. NW,
Washington, DC 20036

Federal Republic of Germany (West
Germany)
4645 Reservoir Rd. NW, Washington,
DC 20007

Ghana
2460 16th St. NW, Washington, DC
20009

Greece
2221 Massachusetts Ave. NW,
Washington, DC 20008

Grenada
1701 New Hampshire Ave. NW,
Washington, DC 20009

Guatemala
2220 R St. NW, Washington, DC
20008

Guinea (Republic of)
2112 Leroy Place NW, Washington,
DC 20008

Guinea-Bissau
E. 43rd St., New York, NY 10017

Guyana
2490 Trace Place NW, Washington,
DC 20008

Haiti
2311 Massachusetts Ave. NW,
Washington, DC 20008

Honduras
4301 Connecticut Ave. NW,
Washington, DC 20008

Hungary
3910 Shoemaker St. NW, Washington, DC 20008

Iceland
2022 Connecticut Ave. NW,
Washington, DC 20008

India
2107 Massachusetts Ave. NW,
Washington, DC 20008

Indonesia
2020 Massachusetts Ave. NW,
Washington, DC 20036

Iraq
1801 P St. NW, Washington, DC
20036

Ireland (Republic of)
2234 Massachusetts Ave. NW,
Washington, DC 20008

Israel
3541 International Drive, NW,
Washington, DC 20008

Italy
1601 Fuller St. NW, Washington,
DC 20009

Ivory Coast
2424 Massachusetts Ave. NW,
Washington DC 20008

Jamaica
1850 K St. NW, Washington, DC
20006

Japan
2520 Massachusetts Ave. NW,
Washington, DC 20008

Jordan
3504 International Dr. NW, Washington, DC 20008

Kenya
2249 R St. NW, Washington, DC
20008

Korea (Republic of)
2320 Massachusetts Ave. NW,
Washington, DC 20008

Kuwait
2940 Tilden St. NW, Washington,
DC 20008

Laos
2222 S St. NW, Washington, DC
20008

Lebanon
2560 28th St. NW, Washington, DC
20008

Lesotho
Caravel Bldg., 1600 Connecticut
Ave. NW, Washington, DC 20009

Liberia
5201 16th St. NW, Washington, DC
20011

Luxembourg
2200 Massachusetts Ave. NW,
Washington, DC 20008

Madagascar
2374 Massachusetts Ave. NW,
Washington, DC 20008

Malawi
1400 20th St. NW, Washington, DC
20036

Malaysia
2401 Massachusetts Ave. NW,
Washington, DC 20008

Maldive Islands
820 Second Ave., Ste. 800C, New
York, NY 10017

Mali
2130 R St. NW, Washington, DC
20008

Malta
2017 Connecticut Ave. NW, Washington, DC 20008

Mauritania
2129 Leroy Place, NW, Washington,
DC 20008

Mauritius
4301 Connecticut Ave. NW, Ste. 134,
Washington, DC 20008

Mexico
2829 16th St. NW, Washington, DC
20009

Monaco
845 Third Ave., New York, NY 10022

Morocco
1601 21st St. NW, Washington, DC
20009

Mozambique
1990 M St., NW, Washington, DC
20036

Nauru (Republic of)
841 Bishop St., Ste. 506, Honolulu, HI
96813

Nepal
2131 Leroy Place, Washington, DC
20008

Netherlands
4200 Linnean Ave. NW, Washington,
DC 20008

New Zealand
37 Observatory Circle NW, Washington, DC 20008

Nicaragua
1627 New Hampshire Ave. NW,
Washington, DC 20009

Niger
2204 R St. NW, Washington, DC
20008

Nigeria
2201 M St. NW, Washington, DC
20037

Norway
2720 34 St. NW, Washington, DC
20008

Oman
2342 Massachusetts Ave. NW,
Washington, DC 20008

Pakistan
2315 Massachusetts Ave. NW,
Washington, DC 20008

Panama
2862 McGill Terrace NW, Washington, DC 20008

Papua New Guinea
1140 19th St. NW, Washington, DC
20036

Paraguay
2400 Massachusetts Ave. NW,
Washington, DC 20008

Peru
1700 Massachusetts Ave. NW,
Washington, DC 20036

Philippines
1617 Massachusetts Ave. NW,
Washington, DC 20036

Poland
2224 Wyoming Ave. NW, Washington, DC 20008

Portugal
2125 Kalorama Rd. NW, Washington,
DC 20008

Qatar
600 New Hampshire Ave. NW, Ste.
1180, Washington, DC 20037

Romania
1607 23rd St. NW, Washington, DC
20008

Russia, Federation of
1125 16th St. NW, Washington, DC
20036

Rwanda
1714 New Hampshire Ave. NW,
Washington, DC 20009

St. Lucia
2100 M St., Ste. 309, Washington, DC
20037

Samoa, Western
3422 Madera Ave., Los Angeles, CA
90039

San Marino
150 E. 58th St., New York, NY 10155

Sao Tome and Principe
801 Second Ave., Ste. 1504, New
York, NY 10017

Saudi Arabia
601 New Hampshire Ave. NW,
Washington, DC 20037

Senegal
2112 Wyoming Ave. NW, Washington, DC 20008

Seychelles
820 Second Ave., New York, NY
10017

Sierra Leone
1701 19th St. NW, Washington, DC
20009

Singapore
1824 R St. NW, Washington, DC
20009

Solomon Islands
3100 Massachusetts Ave. NW,
Washington, DC 20008

Somalia
600 New Hampshire Ave. NW,
Washington, DC 20037

South Africa
3051 Massachusetts Ave. NW,
Washington, DC 20008

Spain
2700 15th St. NW, Washington, DC
20009

Sri Lanka
2148 Wyoming Ave. NW, Washington, DC 20008

Sudan
2210 Massachusetts Ave. NW,
Washington, DC 20008

Suriname
2600 Virginia Ave. NW, Ste. 711,
Washington, DC 20037

Swaziland
4301 Connecticut Ave. NW,
Washington, DC 20008

Sweden
600 New Hampshire Ave. NW,
Washington, DC 20037

Switzerland
2900 Cathedral Ave. NW, Washington, DC 20008

Syria
2215 Wyoming Ave. NW, Washington, DC 20008

Taiwan
801 Second Ave., 9th Fl., New York, NY 10017

Tanzania
2139 R St. NW, Washington, DC 20008

Thailand
2300 Kalorama Rd. NW, Washington, DC 20008

Toga
2208 Massachusetts Ave. NW,
Washington, DC 20008

Transkei
1511 K St. NW, Ste. 611, Washington, DC 20005

Trinidad and Tobago
1708 Massachusetts Ave. NW,
Washington, DC 20036

Tunisia
2408 Massachusetts Ave. NW,
Washington, DC 20008

Turkey
1606 23rd St. NW, Washington, DC 20008

Uganda
5909 16th St. NW, Washington, DC 20011

United Arab Emirates
600 New Hampshire Ave., Ste. 740, Washington, DC 20037

United Kingdom (includes England, Scotland, Wales, and Northern Ireland)
3100 Massachusetts Ave. NW,
Washington, DC 20008

Uruguay
1918 F St. NW, Washington, DC 20006

Vanuatu
3100 Massachusetts Ave. NW,
Washington, DC 20008

Venezuela
2445 Massachusetts Ave. NW,
Washington, DC 20008

North Yemen (Yemen Arab Republic)
600 New Hampshire Ave. NW,
Washington, DC 20037

Yugoslavia (Bosnia, Croatia, Slovenia)
2410 California St. NW, Washington, DC 20008

Zaire
1800 New Hampshire Ave. NW,
Washington, DC 20009

Zambia
2419 Massachusetts Ave. NW,
Washington, DC 20008

Zimbabwe
2852 McGill Terrace NW, Washington, DC 20008

APPENDIX C
Pen Pal Organizations

Pen Pals Unlimited (all ages)
P.O. Box 6283
Huntington Beach, CA 92615

> Send $2.00 and a stamped, self-addressed envelope, along with your name, address, age, sex, hobbies, and interests, and they will match you with someone in the U.S.

Friends Forever Pen Pal Club (Ages 7 to 16)
P.O. Box 20103
Park West Post Office
New York, NY 10025

> Send $3.00 along with your name, address, age, sex, hobbies, and interests.

International Pen Friends (all ages)
P.O. Box 290065
Brooklyn, NY 11229-0001

> Send a stamped, self-addressed envelop with a request for information. They match pen pals of all ages and interests from around the world. Cassette and exchange programs are available for children with disabilities, including blindness. They publish their own magazine.

World Pen Pals (Ages 12 to 20)
1690 Como Avenue
St. Paul, MN 55108

> Send a business-sized, self-addressed, stamped envelop to receive an application OR send a letter with $3.00, SASE, and name, age, sex, and languages you know and countries where you already have pen pals. You will receive the name of a pen pal in another country, a newsletter, and suggestions for letter writing.

Student Letter Exchange (Ages 9 to 16)
Waseca, MN 56093

> Teachers can send a stamped, self-addressed envelop along with a request for information.

CONTRIBUTORS

J. LEON BOLER is a middle school science teacher in Minneapolis. He is author of the highly acclaimed simulation *Nuclear Escape*.

WALTER ENLOE serves as the director of Outreach in the Institute of International Studies, University of Minnesota. He is also the assistant to the director of the institute. From 1971 to 1980 he taught kindergarten through twelfth grade at Paideia School in Atlanta, and from 1980 to 1988 he taught at and was principal of Hiroshima International School.

DOROTHY HOFFMAN is a primary teacher at Ramsey International Fine Arts School in Minneapolis. She has written outstanding curricula in the areas of multicultural and global education.

LARRY JOHNSON teaches storytelling and video production in the Minneapolis public schools. Larry and his wife, Elaine, won Grand Prize at the first Tokyo International Video Festival.

CHARLES KILPATRICK is a geography educator and computer specialist in California. He is a consultant to the National Geographic Society.

TODD PIERSON teaches sixth grade at the Pillsbury Math and Science School in Minneapolis. Todd is an active member of Educators for Social Responsibility.

PETER RICHARDS is a primary teacher at the Paideia School in Atlanta. He presents workshops around the United States on helping children become archaeologists and anthropologists of their locales.

KEN SIMON teaches social studies at the St. Paul Academy in the Twin Cities. In 1992, Ken was selected to be a Mondale Fellow at the H. H. Humphrey Center for Public Affairs at the University of Minnesota.

HILARY STOCK is a social studies specialist for the Wisconsin Department of Public Instruction. She is a director of the Great Lakes–Japan-in-the-Schools Project.

MEG LITTLE WARREN is currently a project consultant to Childreach (formerly Foster Parents Plan), an internationally respected humanitarian organization linking personal sponsors with individual needy children and their families overseas. She is a specialist in children's art.

Celebrate Our Multicultural World

FOLKTALES
Teaching Reading through Visualization and Drawing
by Laura Rose (1992)

Invite your students into reading and imagining with folktales from Russia, Japan, Denmark, West Africa, and the Ojibway and other peoples. Each story offers a drawing page along with each page of text.

Grades K-5.
128 pages, 8 1/2" x 11", softbound.

ZB29-W . . . $15.95

FOLKTALES AUDIOTAPES
Teaching Reading through Visualization and Drawing
by Laura Rose (1993)

You can use these cassettes with all the teaching options of the book *Folktales*. Set up centers for listening, drawing, and using the imagination.

Grades K-5.
Five audiotapes, with one complete story on each side.

ZA03-W . . . $32.95

CHANGING OUR WORLD
A Handbook for Young Activists
by Paul Fleisher (1993)

Here's a practical, step-by-step guide that offers a wide range of options for action . . . and gives students specific suggestions to help them get organized.

Grades 7-12.
236 pages, 8 1/2" x 11", softbound.

ZB34-W . . . $31.95

JOINING HANDS
From Personal to Planetary Friendship in the Primary Classroom
by Rahima Carol Wade (1991)

Create a caring classroom community with these 154 easy-to-use activities. This interdisciplinary and multicultural unit integrates well into your existing curriculum or stands as a separate unit.

Grades PreK-3.
224 pages, 8 1/2" x 11", softbound.

ZB19-W . . . $19.95

To order, write or call—

Zephyr Press
P.O. Box 13448-W
Tucson, Arizona 85732-3448
Phone—(602) 322-5090
FAX—(602) 323-9402

You can also request a free copy of our current catalog showing other learning materials that foster whole-brain learning, creative thinking, and self-awareness.